FITNESS FOR THE MIND AND BODY

TAI CHI

FITNESS FOR THE MIND AND BODY

TAI CHI

LORETTA M. WOLLERING

ROSEN
PUBLISHING

New York

Published in 2015 by The Rosen Publishing Group, Inc.
29 East 21st Street, New York, NY 10010

© 2015 Hinkler Books

First Edition

Library of Congress Cataloging-in-Publication Data

Wollering, Loretta.
  Tai chi/Loretta M. Wollering. — First Edition.
      pages cm. — (Fitness for the mind and body)
  Includes bibliographical references and index.
  ISBN 978-1-4777-8166-1 (library bound)
  1. Tai chi for children—Juvenile literature. I. Title.
  GV504.6.C44W65 2015
  613.7'148—dc23

2014023906

Manufactured in the United States of America

A note on spelling: Many sources spell the art "tai chi chuan," using the Wade-Giles method of romanization. The method now used in China, and therefore in all current print dictionaries, colleges, and bilingual documents is the pinyin romanization method. As such, although the pronunciation is the same (tie jee chwenn), the term *tai chi chuan* should be written in our Latin alphabet as *taijiquan*, and as it is not a proper noun, it should not be capitalized as is so commonly done in error. Nonetheless, the name tai chi chuan has become so common that it will appear as such throughout this book.

Always do the warm-up exercises before attempting any individual exercises. It is recommended that you check with your doctor or healthcare professional before commencing any exercise regime. While every care has been taken in the preparation of this material, the publishers and their respective employees or agents will not accept responsibility for injury or damage occasioned to any person as a result of participation in the activities described in this book.

Contents

Chen Style

Enhancing Tai Chi

Tai Chi Challenge

What is tai chi chuan?

Tai chi chuan, alternately spelled, "taijiquan," is an ancient Chinese martial art with roots in the Taoist philosophy of China, which dates back thousands of years.

Tai chi chuan began as a martial art, but because it incorporates Eastern philosophy into all its practices, it became known as a powerful path to self-development. The core of tai chi is China's oldest philosophical and religious tradition, called Taoism. In and of itself, Taoism is not a religion, but a way of seeking to understand the world and how we are a part of it. It looks to the patterns of nature within and without, noting how they connect the whole universe.

According to Taoism, the more we align ourselves with the patterns of nature and ride the ebbs and tides of the universe's current, the more we will be at peace and the stronger we will become—being closer to our source and its energy. So as much as tai chi begins as a physical practice, it becomes a metaphysical practice as well.

Chop wood, carry water

A famous Zen Buddhist story sums up the approach of tai chi: When the student asked the master what is the path to enlightenment, the master replied, "Chop wood, carry water." And so it is with tai chi—we enter the gate with little more

than basic physical exercises and mind-quieting techniques. But it is how we do them, how we meditate on them, how we let them change us as we change them—this is what finally brings us to the threshold of a restructured body and a developed spirit.

Though it is fast gaining popularity in the Western world, many of us still do not understand what tai chi is or how it could possibly be a martial art as well as a healing art. Most people liken it to "moving yoga" or dance-like moving meditation. This far underestimates and overgeneralizes what tai chi is and the power it is capable of generating. Much of this misunderstanding is due to the fact that tai chi is a highly internalized and subjective practice and experience. The closest most of us ever get to tai chi is a few weeks or months of an introductory class geared to the casual observer. As is the case with merely chopping wood and fetching buckets of water, it feels like and appears to be nothing more than mundane actions.

A misunderstood art

One reason people misunderstand the breadth and depth of tai chi practice is the many popular tai chi classes, videos, and programs that are geared toward senior citizens or people challenged with physical degradation, such as arthritis. Tai chi's flexible nature proves it to be one of the best physical therapies for such conditions, especially since this practice of tai chi is very gentle. Yet the art is so much more than that. Tai chi practice is not just for those with debilitating health conditions or the aged.

In "tai chi for health" or "tai chi as moving meditation" applications, the focus is on slowing the movements down as much as possible and cultivating an intense focus on one's thoughts and movements. When solely exposed to this kind of training, one can only wonder, "How can this be a martial art? What do they do, fight in slow motion?" And the answer to that is: "No, they don't fight in slow motion, and although the training for tai chi in martial arts may involve these slow meditative movements, it also involves very intense training that you don't commonly see. And yes, some of it is fast."

The second half of this book will introduce you to swifter means of practicing tai chi—experiment with these postures if you are athletic and have no injury. It is a little taste of what a more intensive tai chi practice is and what might be done in a class that teaches tai chi for martial arts.

Is *tai chi chuan* the same as *taijiquan*?

There are two popular ways of transliterating Chinese characters into the Latin alphabet (the alphabet used for most Western languages). The pinyin method is the one in current use, and the Wade-Giles method is an older way that China and the academic, political, and business worlds no longer use.

The martial art was introduced to the Western world, however, in its Wade-Giles spelling of "tai chi chuan," and this is the spelling we are used to reading and writing. Pinyin writes tai chi chuan as "taijiquan," and you will increasingly see this version. Keep in mind, though, that it is still the same thing, just a different way of transliterating. And no matter how you write it, never pronounce *quan* as "kwan," as you would in English. The proper pronunciation is "tie gee chwenn."

on the inside. This style of tai chi works intensively on the *qi* development, as well as the connective tissues that bind the body and all its fibers together.

A secret art

For more than a century, Chen Style remained a closely guarded secret, passed only from one family member to another. The reason for the secrecy is twofold. For one, because the way of tai chi was originally a combat art, teachers were wary about to whom they wanted to reveal such secrets. At that time, warfare, muggings, and gang violence were accomplished through hand-to hand combat, and no one wanted to teach a potential opponent how to fight more efficiently.

The second reason for keeping the way of tai chi secret is that teachers did not want to waste their time and energy on passing along information to individuals incapable of comprehending or appreciating the art or those incapable of maintaining the necessary self-discipline for the deep

An ancient practice

The oldest documented form of tai chi—Chen Style—can be practiced gently for healing and restructuring, but its traditional practice was intensive martial training. The Chen family was a military clan that incorporated tai chi principles into their family-style kung fu hand-to-hand combat. Some historians believe that the Chen family originated tai chi chuan, while other historians believe that the Chen family learned tai chi principles through the student lineage of a 12th-century Taoist hermit named Zhang San Feng. One thing is for certain: all other forms of tai chi originated from the Chen Style.

Chen Style

In communist China, there has been dispute about whether Zhang San Feng was an actual historical figure or is a collection of legends. Modern China's current stance is that tai chi chuan originated with the Chen family during the latter half of the 1600s, when it was first formally documented. The choreographed set of movements, known as a "tai chi form" can be first traced to this military family.

Chen Style involves a lot of rotation, rooting, and structural work. This makes it an excellent practice for hand-to-hand combat while also making it a practice that can rebuild the body from the inside out. Following a Chen Style regimen builds such incredible endurance and strength that many practitioners of this style are said to be like "steel wrapped within cotton"—the practitioners and their movements look simple and soft on the outside, with the inner strength, mastery of tai chi principles, and fortitude concealed deeply

Tai chi fans

Tai chi group outdoor performances often feature fan sequences. As bright and colorful as these accessories are, they were not originally employed for their aesthetic value. Tai chi fans are really defensive weapons that can block projectiles and even parry hand-held swords. A warrior can easily conceal a folded fan, which can also serve as a club to smash enemies. Demonstration and beginner fans are usually made of nylon or silk with wooden slats. True weapon fans are made with slats of iron or steel—some even feature blades at the end of each fan point.

All in the family

Traditionally, a tai chi chuan form is named after the surname of the family who developed it. As you may know or have figured out, the family name comes first in Chinese names. Along with the classic Chen Style and the current Yang Style, there are more than a hundred various styles of tai chi. The other most "classic" style of tai chi is called the Wu/Hao Style. The Wu family learned from both the Yang and Chen families and contributed to the written Tai Chi Classics. The Wu family then taught the Hao family, who made a few modifications to this style of tai chi. Two other styles are also considered "classical" styles of tai chi: the Sun Style, named after Sun Lutang, and the Northern Wu Style, named after a different Wu family.

Sun Lutang

traditional practice of tai chi. There were no video stores. Books were very rare. The only way to pass on and preserve the art of tai chi chuan was to spend a great deal of time entrusting it to a capable student desiring to grow from the practice and spread it on to select others.

Yang Lu Chan

Finally, in the early 1800s, an event occurred that would change the world of tai chi chuan—the Chen family taught the art to an outsider: Yang Lu Chan.

Yang Lu Chan was one of the few outsiders allowed into the Chen family to learn their tai chi chuan. To prove his character and dedication, before learning anything, Yang stayed on as a farm worker for the Chen family for several years. After he was accepted and learned the Chen Style tai chi chuan forms and methodology, he returned to his hometown and offered to teach tai chi. His openness in sharing tai chi was considered very progressive. Several years later, the royal family in Beijing commissioned him to teach tai chi. This led to tai chi's explosion in popularity in China, and later, throughout the world.

Yang's family preserved the teachings and passed them on, resulting in what became known as Yang Style tai chi chuan. It was Yang Lu Chan's grandson Yang Cheng Fu, however, who standardized the tai chi form and methodology that is commonly practiced now as Yang Style.

Tai chi historians note that the Yang Style widely practiced today is a far gentler practice than that first taught by Yang Lu Chan. Yet you can use an in-depth practice of today's Yang Style tai chi for martial arts application, especially in techniques of evasiveness and keeping the opponent off-balance. From the Chen and Yang Styles, numerous other styles of tai chi have emerged and continue to develop.

Something for everyone

As with the practice of yoga, there is no "one" tai chi form practice. There are however, tai chi principles that are common throughout the myriad tai chi forms and teaching methodologies. These principles are said to have been first penned by Zhang San Feng somewhere in the latter Song

Dynasty to the early Ming Dynasty (12th to 14th centuries). Over time, other famous masters added to his teachings.

The physical principles prove time and again that they work, and the metaphysical principles, though far more subjective, have led many practitioners on the path to spiritual enlightenment and power.

The beauty of tai chi, as well as the difficulty of it, is that the principles must drive the practice—you cannot merely mimic a teacher. Tai chi is a kinesthetic gateway to self-development and requires dedication and patience. You must pay attention to what is in your mind and how you choose to manifest that into your body. This book will help you with that by showing the muscles and how they are aligned with each tai chi posture. Take the time to feel the machinery of your body.

Tai chi is heavily concerned with the cultivation of one's structure and developing solid stances, flexibility, and swiftness, so if you wish to train in tai chi, whether for health or for martial arts application, you must first condition your body, essentially restructuring it. Without such discipline, repeated intensive practice or martial arts practice increases your risk of injury. But with tai chi discipline—unlike many martial arts that will eventually wear out the practitioners' joints—tai chi chuan prevents self-injury and hastens healing of existing injuries. This makes the martial artist even more powerful. In this regard, tai chi is like the ultimate "engineering" of the body, using the muscles, bones, and joints in ways that always keep the practitioner in beneficial postures while neutralizing malevolent forces, internal thoughts, and energies.

Zhang San Feng

Two sides of the same coin

In essence, tai chi uses the same knowledge for healing as it does for hurting (combat). As in the Chinese concept of yin and yang, the two are opposite sides of the same coin. If you understand how to position yourself and truly "feel" the difference between advantageous body positioning and disadvantageous positioning, then you can start to understand it in a partner or opponent.

The next step entails learning how to always put the opponent into the most disadvantageous position while using his or her energy to put you in a better position. When the opponent moves fast, you move quickly; when slow, you move slowly. This can only be accomplished with a thorough and consistent self-practice of tai chi, beginning with coordinating and conditioning the physical aspect of oneself. This book introduces you to that basic level. It is the first step that can bring about changes in your health and fitness and can later springboard you to the next level, should you wish to pursue it.

If you are a student enthusiastic to learn tai chi martial arts applications, you must first gain a solid understanding of tai chi's basic principles of structure and energy as it applies to better health. If your "machinery" (your body) is not aligned, strong, and running smoothly, the last thing you want to do is throw it into a combat situation—that will surely result in further injury. What's the point of learning 101 martial arts applications if you spend your golden years hobbling on a cane or sitting in a wheelchair due to joint damage from such practices? Who cares if at one time you could use a tai chi posture 20 different ways to fight . . . think about how is it serving you now.

What does "tai chi chuan" mean?

The name tai chi chuan is commonly translated as "grand ultimate fist" or "supreme ultimate fist," but a better translation of the Chinese characters is: "great polarities martial method." The word *tai* means "grand" or "supreme," and *chi* means "terminus" or "polarities." The word *chuan* literally means "fist," but it more generally implies a martial arts practice. The term *tai chi* comes from Taoist philosophy. In Taoism, the tai chi or "great polarities," refers to the relationship between the two opposite yet harmonious forces of nature known as "yin" and "yang."

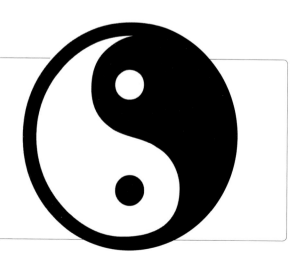

On the other hand, if you are put off by the concept of martial arts, keep in mind that no matter how pacifist your beliefs, your mind and body are always under assault—how will you protect them? Who are such assailants? Why, it's the everyday wear and tear of life. The constant stress of life—the frustrations, the demands, others' angers and hurts, and our own self-defeating thoughts and internal turmoil take a toll both mentally and physically. So even if you have no desire to learn martial applications or engage in sparring, do yourself a favor and use the empowering martial arts philosophy and wisdom garnered from practicing tai chi.

The tai chi diagram

The Taoists created the yin and yang symbol, which is known in China as the "tai chi diagram," or the *tai chi tu* (also written "*taijitu*"). It shows how the extreme of one is the birth of its opposite and how the two are united as a whole through the center point. Just as the days get darker as we approach the winter solstice, darkness eventually passes, and then the days slowly become lighter again. On and on the cycle continues. Two polarities: each one only existing because of the other and continually begetting each other. This is the flow with which you become one in an ever-deepening practice of tai chi chuan.

Homeostasis

The human body continually seeks balance. Chemically, your body is always at work balancing out acids and bases, the gases in your blood, the amount of water in your body, your temperature, your hormone levels, the actions of agonist and protagonist muscle groups; it is in constant flux. Mentally and energetically you feel the need for balance as well: a preponderance of stimuli produces stress, too little produces boredom; the need to feel loved is balanced with the need to provide it. Taoism recognizes all of this as the interplay of yin and yang, and tai chi is a methodology to manifest such balance.

The great polarities

What is yin and yang and why does tai chi so often speak of it? The Taoists say that together, yin and yang is the "mother of all things in the universe." We only know something for its "thing" and the "lack of its thing"—or opposite of it. The positive end of a magnet only exists because there is a negative end. We can only perceive something as light because we know darkness. Something feels cold to us because we know what "warmer" feels like. Left can only exist because we label its opposite as right. While this can lead to conflict, it can also lead to harmony, just like the love between older (a parent) and younger (the child), or the balance of salty and sweet.

Taoism seeks the wise understanding, balancing, blending, and connecting between yin and yang. Tai chi chuan is a Taoist art that involves physical and mental development to come to this growth and enlightenment.

The Chinese characters for yin and yang respectively imply the sunny side of a hill and the shady side of a hill. There is no moral implication about good or bad or positive and negative. It's all relative, depending on the context. In the same way, when things change, as in the earth turning and the sunlight shifting, what was once shady can become light and vice-versa. The light and darkness can continually change.

So do, in a very physical sense, your muscles work in tandem as agonist and protagonist. When one contracts, the other lengthens. The contracting one is doing the prime moving work, but the passive one is supporting it so that it can do what it needs to do with balance. And finally, to move in the opposite direction, the agonist and protagonist switch roles. Physical therapists and personal trainers must have an acute awareness of the yin and yang of their clients' muscles and how to maintain proper balance for optimal performance.

Tai chi and your health

An effective way to get fit and healthy, tai chi chuan is fast becoming a global superstar in the fields of integrative and holistic medicine.

Even the most highly regarded medical schools and establishments, which are usually quite skeptical and conservative in nature, consistently bestow accolades upon the practice of tai chi. "The Health Benefits of Tai Chi," a 2009 Harvard University Medical School publication[1], for example, suggests that the popular moniker of tai chi, "meditation in motion" could just as well be "*medication* in motion." As an adjunct therapy used together with primary medical treatments, tai chi can effectively help treat or prevent many health problems.

"The Health Benefits of Tai Chi" also cites further medical studies that showed tai chi can successfully improve muscle strength, flexibility, balance, and aerobic conditioning, as well as maintain bone density in post-menopausal women and lower blood pressure. It also has shown potential for improving the quality of life and functional capacity for those suffering from arthritis, heart disease, and Parkinson's Disease. That is powerful medication in motion.

Studies in China are even more numerous and cover a far wider range of health issues improved by the practice of tai chi chuan. Most of the medical studies have demonstrated significant improvements in overall health with just three months of consistent practice. Can you imagine what a year or a lifetime of consistent tai chi activity could do?

Studies of the health benefits of tai chi for the physical body have consistently yielded positive results. This has led to numerous organizations sponsoring or endorsing tai chi programs. For example, in the United States, the National Multiple Sclerosis Society offers tai chi classes to those challenged with multiple sclerosis and several arthritis foundations endorse tai chi and tai chi programs specifically geared for this condition.

Exercise for the mind

Tai chi is also gaining the attention of psychological health researchers as well. One article, published in the *Journal of Alternative and Complementary Medicine*[2] cites evidence of how tai chi can help treat psychological issues. This particular

Do-it-yourself healthcare

Now as in the past, tai chi's adherents use it as a sort of "do-it-yourself" healthcare program. Clinical studies are now demonstrating the physical and psychological benefits that you can attain by following a consistent regimen of tai chi.

Though no holistic health or fitness method can overcome ongoing unhealthy lifestyle choices, many people report that a dedicated tai chi practice has made it easier and more enjoyable for them to stay committed to healthy mind-body habits long into their senior years, thereby greatly improving the quality of their lives.

Yet, tai chi chuan is not a quick fix; it can take several weeks to several months to realize significant effects. Your patience and faith in yourself will be rewarded once you understand that you will get out of it what you put into it.

What the Chinese knew all along

Other intense martial arts, such as kung fu, will eventually cause wear and tear on the practitioner's body, but the Chinese found the opposite was true of tai chi chuan practice. The more people practiced tai chi—whether for martial arts or merely physical exercise—the stronger they seemed to become. Their prior injuries improved, and they became more limber and flexible with age, instead of sicker and weaker. This is what led to the explosion of tai chi's popularity in China—an emerging nation that relied on self-care and natural methods to treat ills. Because tai chi works the entire body and mind at every instant, it is a very effective and time-efficient way to improve overall wellness.

article suggested tai chi as an effective treatment for post-traumatic stress disorders experienced by survivors of torture and refugee trauma. The Taoist influence of tai chi focuses on helping one to learn how to let go and relax into challenge.

Taoists also recognize the concept of *qi* as the life force energy that permeates us, as well as the universe. Tai chi is said to balance this energy. When the entire body is exercised in a balanced manner, along with balancing the mind, the life force energy flows unhindered. This is said to help release ill health and mental trauma, leading to improved physical health and psychological peace.

An alternative to other mind-body exercises

You may wish to practice a mind-body exercise such as yoga or Pilates but are discouraged because of physical limitations or restrictions. Maybe you cannot lie on the floor due to back surgery or breathing problems. Tai chi can provide the solution. Even in those of us with debilitating conditions, tai chi can lead to health improvements. For example, a 2012 Sydney University Study[3] demonstrated that tai chi significantly improved balance, exercise capacity, muscle strength, and the quality of life for people living with chronic obstructive pulmonary disease.

Holding your head down for long periods of time can wreak havoc on your balance if you suffer from vertigo, and certain deep or wide knee bends are impossible for some of us. Wearing a prosthetic or having rods in your spine can prevent you from engaging in back bends, leg bends, and many other

exercise moves found in yoga and Pilates. Tai chi, which you can tailor to suit your individual strengths and weaknesses, could be the perfect alternative for you.

Check with your doctor

If you are facing any of these challenges, please consult your doctor about tai chi. Remember that anything you see within this book can be customized by you, your doctor, or physical therapist to suit your needs. If there are any exercises listed here that your doctor recommends that you avoid, simply omit them. As the knowledge of tai chi continues to spread, you will be sure to hear more doctors supporting it and more physical therapists finding ways for their special-needs clients to benefit from it.

[1] "The Health Benefits of Tai Chi." *Harvard Women's Health Watch* (May 2009).

[2] Grodin, Piwowarczyk, Fulker, Bazazi, and Saper. "Treating Survivors of Torture and Refugee Trauma: A Preliminary Case Series Using Qigong and Tai Chi." *Journal of Alternative and Complementary Medicine* (September 2008): 14(7) 801–806.

[3] Leung, McKeough, Peters, and Alison. "Short-form Sun-style Tai Chi as an exercise training modality in people with COPD." *European Respiratory Journal* (August 2012).

Tai chi at home

The only tool or equipment you need to do tai chi is your own body. Add to that comfortable clothes and perhaps a few square feet of space, and you are ready to go.

Tai chi is ideally performed outdoors, so if you have a backyard or garden, make the most of a natural setting. Still, for those who lack outside space or just want to practice in private, it is easy to create a suitable tai chi space inside your home.

Finding room

Move some furniture out of the way and get as much empty floor space as possible—a long narrow space will work better than a square one. Even in small spaces, though, you can do tai chi movements—simply reposition yourself back into place when you run out of room. Remember this: high-level tai chi masters have to keep up with their practice. Many of them travel for seminars and conferences and stay in hotel rooms. They don't let that small-space issue get in the way of their practice, so neither should you.

Tai chi and music

Silence can enhance your tai chi experience, but so too can music. Some practitioners feel that it improves their focus. If you like the idea of background music, try practicing your tai chi with gentle "new age" type music, soft classical music, or ambient nature sounds. It's usually best to avoid music that contains singing because the lyrics might distract you. If you live in the quiet countryside, you may enjoy the "music" of nature right outside your window. Whether you opt for music or silence, your goal is to keep an internal focus rather than an external one. After much meditative practice, even noise will not disturb your tai chi practice.

Sounds

A quiet environment is conducive to your tai chi practice. Turn off the TV and your MP3 player, close doors to noisy rooms, and practice at the quietest time of the day, early in the morning, if possible. If you live in a noisy neighborhood or there is construction noise outside, consider purchasing earplugs or a hearing-protection headset. You may not be able to control your environment outside, but don't let that stop you. Think of how you can control it inside.

Air

The Chinese tai chi masters advise that it's best to have plenty of fresh air during your practice. Cooking odors and fumes from paint or carpeting are not healthful. Open your windows to rid your space of any stale air before or during your practice. You may also want to invest in a good air purifier and ionizer to provide you with a fresh place to enjoy your tai chi practice.

Timing

Traditionally, the Chinese believe that tai chi is best practiced early in the morning, just before or during sunrise. This is the time you can absorb the most energy from the universe, and your body can develop the fastest.

Tai chi is also a great way to start your day off with "good energy." If arising at dawn deprives you of necessary sleep, set your alarm early, practice your tai chi, and then take a nap. Napping after a tai chi workout is an excellent way to encourage healing and rejuvenation.

Steady on your feet

You can practice tai chi barefoot or in sneakers, but any comfortable, flat, flexible, and ground-gripping shoe will work. There are a multitude of speciality tai chi shoes, but many students wear the traditional black martial arts–type practice shoe or Chinese cloth mary janes, which are quite inexpensive.

If early-morning is impossible, practice tai chi in the afternoon or evening. You can also split up your practice throughout the day—tai chi need not be completed in one block. Just be sure to avoid doing anything stimulating right before bedtime, such as the plyometric sequences. The closer to bedtime you practice, the slower and more meditative your practice should be. And wait at least a half hour before or after meals before practicing tai chi, and ensure that you are well hydrated before and after practice.

Mixing it up

Practicing in your home is pleasant, because it is a familiar environment in which you feel safe and comfortable. Yet, over time, familiarity may lead to a sense of ennui, which might limit your development. Practicing outdoors provides you with an ever-changing environment and different surfaces on which to practice. There are things you can do inside your home to create differences in your indoor environment to mimic the changes you would otherwise experience outdoors.

One thing you can do is practice with various footwear. If you wear orthotics or any leg braces, of course first check with your doctor. If you are ready for a change, try wearing socks only one day, then a pair of comfortable shoes the next, and then try going barefoot. Then combine the different footwear with practice on different surfaces. Try it on the carpet or on carpets of different piles. What about bare floors? How does your tai chi feel on the bare floor when you wear socks

versus when you wear sneakers? Don't always stick to what is easy. Challenge yourself by trying different footwear and surfaces.

If you have a limited space, such as a small apartment, hotel room, or dorm room, try facing in different directions when practicing your tai chi. If you have a large house, try practicing in different rooms. Make note of how these different places make you feel, as well as how they physically make it easier or harder to practice. You should be able to do some kind of tai chi practice virtually anywhere as your body and mind become more cultivated and thus adaptable to the environment in which you find yourself.

Using what's in your environment

If you need to hold onto something for your balance, make sure that it is a sturdy piece of furniture. Chests of drawers and tall-backed chairs, for example, provide you with something to hold onto for high stances. Dinner tables and low-backed chairs can help you with medium stances. Coffee tables, sofa seats, trunks, and the lower rungs of chair legs can aid you in steadying yourself in deep stances such as the Yang Style Snake Creeps Down posture. Be creative. Use your environment to assist your practice.

What to wear

The key word for tai chi apparel is *comfort*—you want to put on clothes that allow you complete freedom of movement. The traditional uniform is flowing silk that flutters with each move of its wearer. With light elastic or other gathering at the wrists and ankles that keep it from flopping awkwardly, this uniform becomes a part of you as you move.

You may not want to invest in pricey silks, but any outfit that lets you move unrestrictedly works for tai chi practice. Many other kinds of fitness wear are made of compression fabrics, such as spandex and lycra, but tai chi masters recommend natural fabrics and very loose pajama-like clothing. Cotton, silk, wool, linen, and bamboo fiber fabrics are considered best, but nowadays many tai chi masters and students wear synthetics. Just browse through your closet for something loose and breathable. If you practice in front of a mirror, though, make sure that your clothing isn't so loose that you can't see your movements and alignments.

Outdoor tai chi practice

Find an outdoor space to get the most from your tai chi practice, connecting yourself and your movements to the *qi* life-force energy of nature.

Traditionally and to this day in China, tai chi is practiced outdoors. Early in the morning, practitioners of the art arise and head to parks and plazas to engage in what is often a group activity. Around the globe, you can witness this happening in any large city's Chinatown section. You will also note that many people will do this regardless of the weather.

You can all join in

A quiet corner of your garden, surrounded by trees and flowers and the serenade of bird song, may be the perfect retreat for you when you want to practice your tai chi alone. We all don't have private gardens or backyards, though, so heading to the nearest park may be the answer for you when you want to enjoy an outdoor tai chi session. You can scope out a secluded nook for yourself or join in one of the many groups that gather in parks everywhere to practice together. There is usually no special protocol for joining in a group tai chi sessions, but respect those around you—especially your elders.

From the Taoist point of view, the entire world is your tai chi studio. Opportunities for tai chi practice and self-development are infinite. Of course you still must use common sense when practicing outdoors. Know your limits. If you have trouble with your balance, don't practice in places with uneven terrain, which could lead to falls and injury. Consider wearing protective gear, such as a bicycle

Heavy weather

Taoists forbid outdoor tai chi practice only during electrical storms or any extreme weather, such as blizzards, heavy rain, and windstorms. It's best not to meditate during these times as well.

helmet or knee and elbow pads. Always check with your doctor first, and assume full self-responsibility for your actions. If you have cardiovascular or respiratory issues, be especially careful in very hot or dry weather. Anytime you feel "off" from the environment, stop and take a rest or end your practice session.

Dress for the weather

Dress comfortably for the weather. In colder weather dress to avoid chill. If you know that the day will start off cool, such as in the early morning, wear layers, such as sweaters, scarves, hats, and gloves, and remove them one by one as the day warms up. Put them back on as you cool down after practice.

In hot weather, dress lightly, in pale colors and loose, breathable fabrics. Be careful about overheating or overexposure to the sun. Sunblock and a hat are always a good idea.

If your heart starts to race or you start to feel ill, get out of the heat but not directly into the extreme of cold air-conditioning. If you are healthy with clearance from your doctor to practice in the hot weather, you will find that over time, your tolerance will increase. In hot climates or during hot weather, it is best is to practice early in the morning or in the evening when the sun has set.

The tai chi masters caution against getting wet, but you may still practice during light rain as long as you wear appropriate waterproof rain gear. Avoid getting damp and chilly or damp and overheated for long periods of time. It will be far better to cease your practice until the weather clears.

Aqua tai chi

The tai chi masters offer an exception to the "don't get damp" rule—the only time you can stay damp while practicing tai chi in when you actually get in the water. So when the temperature rises, head to the beach or swimming pool for a tai chi session. Just make sure to avoid chills when you are done.

Getting in sync with nature

The Taoists believe that practicing outdoors in any weather, except the most extreme, is a good way for the individual to become in sync with the rhythms of nature, thus fostering a sense of inner peace and a strong physical body. They also believe that you can absorb the energy of the atmosphere to give you more *qi* life-force energy.

If you practice in a very humid area or sweat easily, consider bringing a change of clothes. If that's not possible, consider wearing moisture-wicking fabrics and apply absorbent talcum powder all over your body before dressing for practice. Bring a towel along to dry yourself off. Be sure to drink enough water to stay well hydrated.

Fuel for the weather

As important as what you put *on* your body is what you put *in* it. Eating and drinking properly will help you get the most from your tai chi practice, no matter what the weather.

Before and after practicing outside in cooler weather, avoid drinking or eating cold or raw foods; the tai chi masters believe that these foods create a yin imbalance in the body.

During a chilly weather practice, you can sip hot organic chicken broth or hot organic vegetable broth. Hot broths are said to be excellent to develop your digestive capacities and help build *qi* energy.

During the hot weather, it is imperative to sip fluids at regular intervals during your tai chi practice. The tai chi masters traditionally drink cool water or diluted tea. Traditional Chinese medicine considers watermelon one of the most cooling foods.

Recipes for success

Along with water, plain tea, and broth, you can brew your own special tai chi beverages that will cool you down in the heat or warm you up in the cold, as well as help protect your *qi* energy. You can steep the ingredients and then strain them out, or let them remain at the bottom of your drinking vessel.

Cooling recipe

The following herbs are said to be cooling and soothing for hot weather. Place them into your water or tea and sip the mixture during your practice. Mix and match among the following:

- fresh lemon juice
- fresh lime juice
- crushed mint
- a pinch of fresh ginger
- xylitol
- stevia
- a pinch of sugar
- watermelon

Warming recipe

Using a base of hot tea or hot water, mix and match the following ingredients into your drink:

- one to several spoonfuls of fresh grated ginger
- one to several spoonfuls of cayenne pepper
- one to several spoonfuls of cinnamon
- black pepper (use sparingly)
- carrot juice
- a little bit of fresh lemon or orange juice
- cloves (again, use sparingly)
- a pinch of brown sugar, honey or other sweetener

Tai chi and nutrition

To get the most from your tai chi practice, you must eat healthily. Like all healthy diets, the best tai chi diet includes lean proteins, whole grains, and plenty of fresh vegetables.

Nutrition is a way of life for the Chinese. Every herb and every food is said to have some special property. Many foods even have an energetic significance.

Naturally good

For centuries, the Chinese people—from the poor uneducated farmer to the worldly business merchant—had an understanding of the energy of the food they ate. Sadly, this understanding of food is becoming lost as more and more Chinese turn away from their old wisdom in favor of modern Western influence and its "engineered" foods.

All Taoist and tai chi–based knowledge and application of herbology and nutrition was founded on the use of organically grown foods free of genetic engineering. As such, you should seek out food that is as close to this natural state as you are able. Processed readily available foods, though convenient, are not good for your well-being, according to the advice of traditional Chinese medicine.

The tai chi diet

The tai chi diet recommended for optimal health is a simple one: mostly fresh vegetables, a carbohydrate base, a little bit of meat, some fat, and very small amounts of sweets and fruits. Beverages should not be ice cold. Diluted plain tea (without sugar) is freely consumed throughout the day. This diet has kept people slim and full of energy for centuries.

When choosing your carbohydrate base, look for whole-grain foods, such as brown rice, barley, and quinoa, and be sure your pasta, noodles, and breads are made from unprocessed flour. Buy fresh, locally grown vegetables in season. Steam them or stir-fry them in a vegetable oil, such as sesame or sunflower oil. For extra flavor add beans, nuts, seeds, or tofu and sprinkle them with a natural soy sauce, such as tamari or shoyu. For meat-eaters, fish, poultry, and seafood are best.

To satisfy a craving for sweets, opt for a serving of fruit. When buying fruit, look for locally grown fresh items like apples and berries or stock up on dried dates, golden raisins, raisins, and figs. Avoid all unrefined sugar, and consume organic honey in moderation.

Start the day right

Tai chi masters all recommend a light, nutritious breakfast. Consume your biggest meal in the first half of the day: breakfast, brunch, or lunch. Eat a light but nutritious dinner, and be sure it is not too close to bedtime.

Fats

The low-fat or even no-fat dietary trend started in America; the traditional Chinese diet does not promote a fat-free trend, and includes both animal and vegetable fats.

Allopathic and holistic physicians alike are beginning to endorse the consumption of "healthy fats"—something that tai chi masters have known for years. While an overabundance of heavy animal fats in your diet is unhealthy, fresh oils, fish fats, and certain other fats are essential for hormone creation and balanced health. Getting healthy fats in your diet actually curbs your appetite. Note too, that most prepared "low fat" foods are high in sugar and other carbohydrates. This can upset your blood sugar balance, which then leads to fat deposition in your body and increased appetite.

Eating with the seasons

Like tai chi, your diet serves you best when it brings you in harmony with the rhythms of nature. Find out what vegetables and fruits are in season when you grocery shop. Eating foods that are in season within your local area is better for your *qi* energy—and cheaper too.

Rice or wheat?

China is known for its main meal staple—rice. The Chinese have eaten white rice for many centuries, whereas other Eastern cultures, such Japan, tend to eat more brown rice. Rice makes up the base of the meal. If you have insulin sensitivity, however, cut down on the rice and bump up the vegetable intake instead.

Although rice is considered the main staple in China, it does not grow well in the north; therefore, wheat has long been the meal staple in northernmost China. Wheat made into noodles, patties, and special steamed buns called *mantou* has traditionally been part of most meals. These days, however, the wheat we eat is genetically very different than the wheat that was traditionally eaten in China (and the rest of the world) for millennia. An ever-increasing number of Western doctors, as well as traditional Chinese medicine doctors, are cautioning people to cut out high wheat consumption, as it has been linked to an explosion of obesity and insulin resistance.

Avoid the ice

Traditionally in China, cold drinks are considered bad for the organs of digestion and to diminish the *qi* energy. Unlike Western styles of exercise in which ice-cold water or other cold beverages are encouraged, tai chi masters recommend consuming drinks that are warm or at room temperature. Cold drinks are only permissible in hot weather or when an individual remains feeling hot for long periods of time.

Eat simply

Again, the goal is to eat "as close to nature" as possible. Eat simply, consuming as few processed foods as possible. Eat more vegetables if you need to control your weight and remove constipation. Eat more protein and fats if you need to gain weight or more muscle mass or to diminish your appetite. Use sweet and raw foods in moderation. Try testing your response to wheat by eliminating it for a while. Get used to having no ice in your drinks. Give your new eating habits at least two weeks minimum, and then experiment further with your diet. Your tai chi practice will help you become more intuitive to sense what is best for you—instead of letting your tongue dictate all your desires!

Advice for vegans and vegetarians

Chinese Buddhists have perfected the art of vegan cooking, yet the biggest problem traditional Chinese medicine doctors observe in vegans and vegetarians is that they often eat "too yin." Too many raw and cold-energy foods, fruits sweets, and starches either lead to a too-thin physique with lack of vitality or a bloated physique with fatigue or underactive thyroid issues. Soy is the main food source of necessary protein for vegans. Be careful and ensure that you look for organic and non-genetically modified soy food products. Also try cutting down on wheat, keeping in mind that many soy sauces and flavorings use wheat derivatives. Other sources of proteins are nuts and amaranth grain. Vegans and vegetarians should consider adding more "yang food" to their diet, such as root vegetables, foods cooked for short amounts of time at high temperatures and healthy fresh oils (as in stir-fried foods), hot pepper, garlic, onions, ginger, scallions, bitter herbs and vegetables, and vegetables that grow in colder climates. These will help increase the internal "fire" of one's energy.

The dantian

In tai chi, the dantian is considered your center of energy and center of gravity. Cultivating an awareness of your dantian is essential to mastering the art of tai chi chuan.

As you begin to learn tai chi chuan, you'll hear much talk about the "center." You are told to move from your center, to guard your center, and to be centered. Yet so few people understand where their center is, what it is, and why it is important in tai chi.

Ask a roomful of people to place their hand where they believe their center lies. Most of them will place it on their heart area, while some on their head and some on their solar plexus. Almost no one places a hand on the lower abdomen—yet this is our true center. This is the very special area from which we must move and center ourselves in tai chi. The old Tai Chi Classics refer to this area as the "dantian."

Internal alchemy

The dantian is an area inside the body that is situated in the lower abdomen, below the navel and the lower back. It is not a physical thing—not a bone or organ—but instead a field. In fact, the Chinese character for *tian* means "field," as in a field of crops that grow vast amounts of the food that nourishes us. The dantian can also be likened to an energy field, much like a force field or magnetic field with moveable and invisible boundaries, yet contained within a certain area.

The word *dan* is a little more complicated to understand and requires a bit of knowledge of Chinese history. The literal translation of the Chinese character for *dan* means "cinnabar," which is a common ore of mercury.

In the East, this bright vermilion mineral was once highly regarded and believed to have magical powers. Exquisite jewelry was crafted from it, and it formed the base of the most expensive cosmetics for the ladies of the court, who applied it to their lips, cheeks, and fingernails. The famous lacquerware of the Song Dynasty utilized this beautiful metal ore.

Old Chinese alchemy—a precursor to our modern-day medicine and chemistry—used cinnabar in elixir compounds for the pursuit of longevity, spiritual power, and immortality.

Despite its beauty, mercury-based cinnabar proved toxic, and those who mined or worked with it often fell ill or died from heavy-metal poisoning. Taoists nonetheless poetically employed the term from chemical and herbal alchemy as a metaphor for practices of "internal alchemy." The Taoists noted that we have our own internal chemicals and that if "processed" in special ways, they can lead to longevity, better moods, greater vitality, and excellent health. They

Adjust your center

Understand that there is always an attraction between your dantian and the earth's dantian (center of gravity). To optimize this energetic attraction, seek to line up your body with the straight line of gravity. This will optimize your tai chi so that it is always adjusting your muscles, joints, spine, and internal organs so that they remain in alignment. Like the wheels of a car, keeping good alignment reduces or eliminates damage from the wear and tear of your daily activities. As you practice the stances, sense how you are positioning your body both above and below your dantian.

named the lower abdominal area of the body the "elixir field" or "dantian," because this was thought to be the area where one's life force—or *qi*—emanated.

Qi energy

The *qi* energy is said to be the thing that keeps us alive. It is the summation of biochemical and physiological processes that are our very life functions. The ancient Taoists believed, much like our modern-day physicists, that the energy in the universe cannot be destroyed—it is everywhere and can be focused. If one loses *qi* due to illness or destructive living habits, one can always recover it again.

Tai chi chuan is one Taoist methodology that helps the body and mind become effective at recovering *qi energy*, storing it, and using it more efficiently. The *qi* is said to travel in concentrated currents along meridian lines, which acupuncturists tap into in order to balance these currents.

The dantian is like an ocean of *qi* in the human body, and much of this comes from the fact that you manifested into human form from the dantian out. If you look at the top of your dantian on the front

of your body, you will see your navel, which is the scar of where your umbilical cord was when you were a fetus. The umbilical cord forms quickly in fetal development and contains two arteries that pump waste-product blood from the body of the fetus to the mother's placenta and one vein that receives oxygen and nutrient-rich blood from the placenta. Once the blood is received by the fetus, it is pumped throughout its body. It is this natural phenomenon that allows one to manifest from a collection of tissue cells into a full-fledged independent human being. When the cord is severed at birth, the ancient Taoists believe that we are still connected to the *qi* of the universe via our dantian.

Our center of gravity

The Taoists' energy-based way of regarding the dantian as the center of our life-force energy may be a metaphysical one, but a very physical definition will also show that this is true. Open an anatomy textbook and you will discover that this area of the adult human body is also its center of gravity. It is the balancing point of our body mass.

Just as in mechanical engineering, knowing the center of gravity of an object allows us to structure it in a way that moves it the most efficiently and wastes the least amount of energy. What if you learned to make use of your center of gravity whenever you moved? What could you do with the extra energy saved? Could it be used for healing, more vitality, more longevity? Pay attention to how your center of gravity is situated in tai chi and you will discover for yourself.

Footwork and hand forms

The secret to making it easy is in the feet. Take the time to master the key stances and steps that make up just about every tai chi chuan posture.

Tai chi is only as solid as its foundation. You can have a building made of steel and concrete, but if it sits on a foundation of sand, it can fall down faster than a hut made of straw. So too it is with your tai chi stances and steps. Your understanding of them builds a strong foundation for your tai chi practice.

Follow the patterns

There are hundreds of tai chi postures that look vastly different from one another. But if you look closely, you will observe that there are just a few steps or stances—terms that are used interchangeably in tai chi—that are common to the postures. If you master these simple footwork patterns, it will be very easy for you to learn tai chi and execute it with ease and grace.

Static stances and steps

The following six stances—horse stance, empty stance, rooster stance, L-stance, tiger stance, and bow-and-arrow stance—are static in nature. They flow into one another by transitioning between them.

Yin and yang of stances

Every stance has its yin and yang aspects. This is something that tai chi martial artists must first master in themselves and then learn to recognize and manipulate in their opponents. The metaphysical implication here is that for every strong or advantageous situation you find yourself in, remember that there is a vulnerable aspect there are well. The "yang," or strength, of the horse stance is on the vertical axis and the horizontal axis. The "yin," or lack of structural strength, is on the fore and aft axis.

Horse stance

Horse stance is the first step for all beginners. This is the most common stance of tai chi, as well as all martial arts. In Chinese, its name is *ma bu*. It is called "horse" stance because correctly done, you feel as if you are sitting on a large horse, even though you are standing.

It is a very customizable stance—you can vary how high or low you wish to "sit" and how far to turn in your toes or flare them out from your leg at the hip joint. For men, your toes should point more forward. For women, your toes will point a little more outwards due to the flare of the pelvis situating the hip socket differently than in males. If your knees hurt, simply take a higher stance and make it narrower by positioning your feet closer together.

To execute horse stance, place your feet apart and parallel to each other, imagining that you are sitting atop a horse. "Sit" into the stance by relaxing your hips and pelvis, while keeping your back straight. Slightly tuck your chin, and raise the top back part of your head toward the sky. Keep your ears in line with your shoulders.

Get it right

Keep your spine straight with no sway in the lower back. Your head must sit straight on your spine with your ears in line with your shoulders. Feel as if the top, back part of your head is suspended from above by a large helium balloon, and that an anchor is dropped from your perineal area straight into the earth. This is said to raise your spirit and root your *qi* energy. Make sure that your knees are turned slightly outward, in line with your toes and not buckling inward. Look in a mirror or take a photo of yourself with a camera autotimer setting. You should be straight with shoulders down, pelvis lightly tucked without leaning back, and knees in line with the toes.

In the traditional practice of tai chi, this stance was often held for several minutes to an hour as a form of standing meditation. If doing so, make yourself relax into the stance as best as possible without losing good structure. This not only strengthens your stabilizer muscles, but it also tones your legs and their tendons and ligaments.

Progressive relaxation

As you maintain this stance, progressively relax yourself from head to toes, all the while re-correcting your structure. Start with your head. Feel the top of it pull toward the heavens. At

Head first

Fight the urge to lean your head too far forward when you are in any tai chi stance. Your head tends to follow your eyes, so you therefore lean forward to do everything from cooking, eating, driving, and reading.

the same time, relax your face. We hold a surprising amount of tension in our facial muscles, and all it does is age us prematurely and block up our energy. So imagine a warm soothing feeling or light wash over you, releasing the worry

lines from your forehead, softening the furrow between your brows, softening and melting your jaw muscles, opening your sinuses and nasal passages . . . and feel your entire scalp soften and relax. Then move this relaxation to your neck and shoulders. As your head rises to the heavens, your shoulders melt downward heavily, and the heaviness exits the base of your fingers as a soothing current of energy. Move the relaxation down your spine and chest, through your torso and pelvis. Take your time. Continue to feel it go down to your thighs, knees, ankles, and feet. Finally, feel it exit your feet into the earth.

Progressive weight sinking

After this, from your shoulders down, feel the mass of your body sinking. Like the sand passing down in an hourglass, feel the weight of your body sink. Let it pass through your legs and finally out your feet into the earth. All the while, your head is gently suspended from above. Your breathing roots down into your abdomen, and your chest remains melted and relaxed. This is the powerful grounding and stabilizing energy of the horse stance.

Like riding a horse

The horse stance is named not only for what it looks like—a person sitting astride a horse—but also for how it functions. In equestrian sports, the posture and movements of the rider influence the movements of the horse. If the rider is unbalanced or exerting pressure somewhere on the horse in an unbalanced manner, the horse will sense this through its center of gravity and move in response. In the same manner, if any of your horse stances are off in tai chi postures, your movements will be unbalanced, and you will not move in the manner you desire. All you need to do is correct your structure, and nature will take care of everything else.

Wuji stance

In tai chi chuan, a narrow horse stance is often called a *wuji*, or "origin," stance.

Empty Stance

After horse stance, which distributes your weight equally between both legs, you begin to learn the stances that vary weight distribution. While most tai chi forms start (and end) with some sort of horse stance, the second move in most tai chi forms is some sort of an empty stance.

A foot or leg is "empty" when there is no added weight on it; your body weight must fully rest on the opposite foot or leg. In an empty stance, the empty foot touches the ground in a relaxed manner. This not only allows for increased variation in mobility, but it also allows the foot to prepare for a kick or other moving leg technique.

An empty stance is narrow in nature, although you can vary how high or low you'd like to sit on the weighted leg, and how widely you'd like to situate the empty foot. There is one rule you don't want to violate: never place the empty foot across the centerline of your body. Imagine a vertical line down the center of the front of your body and continuing down to the floor. Don't place that empty foot across that centerline. To do so would upset your balance and pull your hips out of structure.

Back-weighted empty stance

The most common empty stance is the back-weighted empty stance in which your back leg carries the weight and your front foot is empty. The toes and ball of your front foot may gently touch the ground.

In another version of back-weighted empty stance, the toes of your flexed foot point upward with your heel on the ground.

When you practice the empty stances, use the same progressive relaxation technique you employed in horse stance. Then use the same weight-dropping practice to sense your body weight dropping through the weighted leg.

Rear-wheel drive

You will notice that many tai chi postures begin from a back-weighted empty step, which then shifts the body weight forward into the next move. This is like the concept of a truck utilizing the powerful thrust and torque derived from rear-wheel drive.

From the top of your head to through your foot, you should be like a straight, but relaxed, pillar. Here too, feel as if you are sitting on a high stool. If your balance falters, simply hold onto a sturdy piece of furniture or the wall, and practice letting go for longer periods. If you are patient with this, your empty stance practice will foster a tremendous increase in balance as well as leg strength.

If you have a condition that causes your legs to fatigue easily, simply take sitting breaks between your balance work on the empty stances. If you overdo it and feel sore the next day, take a rest and resume a day or two later. Just do a little less and rest more. This is one of the most effective ways to develop an excellent sense of balance. It can help amputees or people relying on canes and walkers. For athletic folks, it builds far more stability and control in their leg muscles.

A walking stride

The empty leg in front of you should be as far away from the weighted leg as it would be if you were about to step down on the forward empty foot, as when walking. In fact, when you walk, you naturally have an empty stance for a moment until you shift your weight forward on to that foot. Then for a moment, you have a front-weighted empty stance.

Front-weighted empty stance

You may also assume an empty stance with your empty foot slightly behind, or almost next to the weighted foot. This is a front-weighted empty stance. It is not that pronounced in tai chi postures and occurs most often as a transitional movement between other stances.

Tuck it in

Avoid a common structural mistake when you execute a front-weighted empty stance, making sure not to lean too far forward as you stick out your buttocks. This overloads the knees. Don't lean back either; keep your spine perpendicular to the ground.

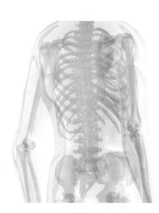

Roll it under

The most common structural mistake seen in the back-weighted empty stance is excess sway in the lower back. Be sure to roll your pelvis under, lean a tiny bit forward from the hips, and retract your head to align your ears with your shoulders.

Practice by walking

A meditative exercise that teaches you about front- and back-weighted empty stances is to simply walk very slowly, noting when you have a back-weighted empty stance and a front-weighted one. Practice correcting your structure at every instant of movement. Practice placing the empty foot forward.

Try it initially with your heel on the ground, and then spend time trying it by first touching the ball of the foot on the ground. Sink on your back-weighted leg to your level of ability and comfort. Then imagine you can roll your weight through the ground and shift onto your forward leg. Flatten your forward foot and take note of your posture and weight-sinking. Do not let the knee of your forward leg extend past your toes. Are you relaxed or are you tensing somewhere? Breathe and adjust your body.

Next, roll your pelvis slightly under and release weight off your back foot. Don't lean forward, but instead align straight with the pull of gravity. Use the rolling of your pelvis to slightly pull in your back leg. You should now find yourself in a forward-weighted empty stance. Bring your back leg up in front of you, sink, and repeat the exercise. It's just like walking, but more mindful. Try narrow stances, wide stances, and long and short paces. Keep your head as if suspended from above, and allow your weight to relax downward with every movement and every pause.

Rooster stance

The rooster stance is like an advanced version of a toes-down back-weighted empty stance. The only difference is that the empty foot is lifted off the floor and the knee is raised to approximately hip height. It is named after how many fowl stand upon one leg with the other lifted for long periods of time. Keep in mind that if one of their legs is raised, the other one remains very rooted.

Nearly every tai chi kick begins with a rooster stance and ends in a rooster stance. The only exception is that most roundhouse-style kicks begin from a twine step.

When kicking, the dantian lifts the thigh into a rooster stance and continues as a whip-like motion through the lower leg and foot. The kick is then immediately pulled into a rooster stance before the next move.

The rooster stance is an excellent stance to use to build an incredible state of balance. Any martial artist or athlete who uses kicks should practice holding the rooster stance for several minutes at a time to heighten control and agility.

Repetitively assuming one rooster stance and then assuming one on the opposite side, also provides the benefits of stretching the lower back, toning the abdominal muscles, and strengthening the hip flexor tendons.

Find the angle

Take a look at the femur, the long bone of the thigh, and you will note that it lies on an angle from the hip area of the femur down to the knee. You preserve this angle when lifting the empty foot into the rooster stance.

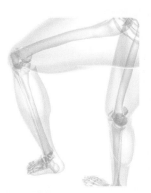

Paying close attention to lining up the inside of your knee with the centerline of your body also increases control and coordination of your leg muscles.

To get into the rooster stance, start with a back-weighted empty stance. Imagine that there is a helium balloon attached by a string to the top of your knee.

Before you begin to lift your knee, relax, and sink into your pelvis. Feel as though you were starting to sit on a high stool. As you "sit" more deeply, allow your knee to lift until your femur is parallel to the floor. For proper structure, be sure that the inside (medial) edge of your knee is in line with your vertical centerline.

Get it right

The most common error people make in rooster stance is to hold the hip of the empty leg too openly. The bent empty leg should be adducted slightly inward. In martial applications, this adduction provides a "shield" to an incoming kick and closes your vulnerable areas if you execute a kick. It also aids your balance, keeping the heavy mass of your leg closer toward your center of gravity (dantian).

Keep your balance

If you have knee pain or balance challenges, substitute a back-weighted empty stance for any rooster stance. Work on improving your balance by lightly holding onto a chair or other solid object as you experiment with lifting your knee. Then try to hold your balance as you let go of the chair for a few seconds. With practice, you'll improve your balance and build strength.

Know your alphabet

Do not inadvertently make a T-stance. To check your position when in an L-stance, look at the back edge of the foot that forms the base of the L. Imagine a perpendicular line shooting straight out from the back of the heel in line with the stem of the L. For example, if your left foot is pointing forward and you are considering it as the base of your L-stance, the line shoots out from the back border of your left heel. When you place your right foot out as the stem of the L, the inside edge of your right heel must never cross over the back-heel line of your base (in this example, left) foot. You can always step the stem back for a wider L-stance. Just ensure that you never cross over that back-heel line of the base foot. Doing so will uproot your balance.

L-stance

As in the horse stance, the L-stance calls for you to firmly plant both feet on the floor, but because your feet point in different directions by 90 degrees, it allows for greater agility than the horse stance.

An L-stance lets you move quickly in a variety of directions. It is often followed by a twist step in the rear foot (page 36) or a front-weighted empty step.

If done correctly, an L-stance can build your balance and rootedness; if done incorrectly, it can hurt your knees or lower back. If you have joint pain or tight adductors, use a narrower L-stance until your flexibility improves. It is imperative that you pay attention to your structure when using this stance.

When in an L-stance, your feet should make the shape of the letter L on the floor. The toes of your front leg (the "stem" of the L) should point out.

Situate your feet 90 degrees to each other, and face your centerline to the center of the stance, neither twisted to the left nor right. An L-stance almost always changes to a bow-and-arrow stance by way of a twist step in the rear leg.

To assume an L-stance, first start in a horse stance with your feet parallel. Sink all your weight straight down onto the left leg so that the right foot is relatively empty. Keep your right heel on the floor and flex your foot so that your toes point upward.

Keeping your weight on the left, outwardly rotate your right hip so that your right toes turn to the right 90 degrees. Allow your torso to slightly turn to the right. Gently tuck your pelvis and sink your weight onto your right foot.

If you do this correctly, your torso is neither in line with the left foot nor the right. Instead, the centerline of your torso should face about 45 degrees from each foot—in the

"middle" of the stance. The leg/foot that you turn out at the hip—in this case, the right leg—forms the stem of the L. The other foot—in this case, the left—forms the base of the L. Now repeat going into L-stance on the other side.

Go high and narrow

Even the slightest of buckling inward of the knees can prove deleterious to your vulnerable knee joints. Solve this by taking a higher and narrower L-stance, and consider stretching your adductors (page 159). Also ensure that you are keeping your pelvis rolled under with no sway in your back. Feel as if you are sitting.

Tiger stance

Throughout tai chi history, tai chi masters have given different names to many of the tai chi stances, depending on region and different tai chi teaching lineages. The tiger stance, though often called "squatting stance," or "squat stance," always looks the same and functions the same. You can do this stance as low as you wish to maximize your workout, or you can do it as a high and narrow stance, which is necessary if you are healing from knee pain or injury.

Tiger stance is the least common stance in tai chi because with its deep squat it is so extreme. It is used martially to evade high hits and to swoop down and uproot or attack an opponent at the ankle or groin area. In tai chi chuan sword forms it is also used for low slices.

For your health, it builds very strong leg muscles, tendons, ligaments, and fascia, and can hasten your explosive (plyometric) strength. This posture is most commonly seen in the Snake Creeps Down posture.

To get into a tiger stance, assume the widest horse stance you can take while still maintaining excellent structure. Shift enough weight off your left leg so that you can pivot on your left heel and outwardly rotate your entire leg—just enough to point your left toes outward approximately 45 degrees or more. Shift your weight back onto your left leg and begin to descend onto the leg. Be sure to keep your left knee facing outward—do not let it turn in.

As you squat down onto your left leg, slide your right foot out, lengthening your right leg and keeping it straight. Your right toes are still pointed forward. Resist the temptation to lean too far forward. Only sink as far down as your body can comfortably accommodate. Your strength and flexibility will increase over time.

With your body weight concentrated on your left leg, you can experiment with turning out your right foot. Notice how

Upright and tucked

As you descend deeper into this stance, you will find that your body will lean a little forward at the hip. This is normal because your center of gravity—your dantian—is sinking and pushing your hip joint in line with, or lower than, your knee. As your pelvis drops, you may find your torso leaning a bit forward, but don't go so deep that you lean forward to the degree that your buttocks raise higher than your center of gravity. When you approach this extreme, not only are you overloading your knees and lower back, but you also destroy your balance. It tips too much mass over your center of gravity. Don't be too eager to go deeply and sacrifice your balance and joint health. Instead, concentrate on keeping your pelvis tucked and your back as upright as possible.

intensively this both stretches and strengthens you. Tiger stance is the most extreme of tai chi stances, so be careful and don't overdo it.

To come out of the stance, imagine that your hips are lifting you upward. Keep your body straight but as relaxed as possible. Repeat on the other side. Hold each stance for a few seconds to a few minutes.

Bow-and-arrow-stance

Bow-and-arrow is another common tai chi chuan stance. Essentially, it is a rooted forward lunge. It is so important for application work and rooting that it is used in virtually every martial art. The art of fencing uses a great variety of lunging stances, but differs greatly from tai chi in that tai chi restrains the forward extension of the body in order to emphasize rootedness. This is also prevents damage to the knee joint.

The bow-and-arrow stance is the complement to the horse stance. Whereas the structural strength of the horse stance is side-to-side, the structural strength of the bow-and-arrow stance is front-to-back. The horse stance is wide laterally, whereas the bow-and-arrow stance is wide longitudinally.

Like the L-stance, a proper bow-and-arrow stance requires that you avoid crossing the back heel line. It should feel stable and comfortable. You can make it as high and narrow as you wish if you have knee pain. If you are athletic, feel free to use a low and deep bow-and-arrow stance. Regardless of your athletic prowess, aim to maintain excellent structure. Don't allow you lower back to sway. Your forward knee must not buckle in, and both feet must remain firmly planted on the ground. Avoid reaching forward.

To get into the bow-and-arrow stance, start by standing with your feet together in a narrow horse stance. Flare out your right foot about 45 degrees or less. This is your base foot. Step out your left foot in front, at a comfortable distance so that both feet can remain on the floor. Make sure your ears

Don't buckle

Make sure that your front leg does not buckle in during a bow-and-arrow stance. Remove any excess sway in your lower back by gently tucking your pelvis, which will also help to tighten your abdominal muscles and keep your abdominal organs in proper alignment.

Check your range

Tai chi beginners usually take too long a step for to begin their bow-and-arrow stances. Here's how to correct it: From the bow-and-arrow stance, keep your back upright as you shift all your weight onto the back leg. Tuck your pelvis, and sit onto your back leg, and ensure that your knee is outward and not twisting inward. Then, let your forward leg's foot flex so your heel remains on the ground and your toes point upward. This should give you a little more range. As long you can keep upright posture and comfortably sit on your back leg, you are okay; if not, you must shorten your stance.

are in line with your shoulders and your pelvis is gently tucked. Lunge about 60 to 70 percent of your body weight forward on your left leg. Keep your left knee in line with your left toes. The farthest you are permitted to lunge is so that the forward leg's knee does not lean past its toes. Exhale, and relax. Feel that you are "sitting" into the posture. Repeat on the other side, ensuring excellence in structure each time.

Dynamic steps

We will now explore the steps and stances of tai chi chuan that are rather dynamic in nature—that is, their purpose is expressed in motion rather than rooting. They also form the transitions between the more static stances.

Whole step

Some tai chi masters argue that there is no such thing as a "whole step" in tai chi, because truthfully every tai chi stance brings you directly into another tai chi stance. The whole step appears to be merely what we do when walking in everyday life, but in tai chi, it is a more mindful movement.

Because it is so similar to everyday walking, when you apply tai chi mindfulness to whole step, you will be reprogramming your body's muscle memory to make your everyday walking more efficient. Whole step is a simple move, but do not

> ## Walking meditation
>
> You can use these steps as a kind of walking *qi* meditation. It is especially soothing to your *qi* and spirit when doing this outdoors, allowing yourself to become very rooted and quiet. Remember that if you have joint pain, you can still do this by simply taking higher and narrower stances. Just sink and root internally, without bending your knees and ankles as much.

assume that its superficial appearance is indicative of its proper execution. Breaking down even seemingly simple movements allows martial artists to better read their opponents. Breaking down movements is also beneficial for fine-tuning the transitions between your stances and steps. This will build more grace and power into your movements.

A whole step should be as long as your natural walking pace. To find it, start walking around, and then suddenly stop. The space between your feet is your natural stride length. As your tai chi practice will lead to increases in strength and flexibility, your stride length for whole step may increase as well. Let it occur naturally.

Whole step connects empty stances to other stances, such as the bow-and-arrow stance. Let's try a simple but mindful exercise in whole step.

Begin with your feet parallel in a narrow horse stance. As you did in the study of horse stance, go through your progressive relaxation and progressive weight-sinking regimens.

Now, step out your left foot emptily on the heel, into a toe-up back-weighted empty stance. Keep your weight sunk on the rear leg and your head erect.

Note that in regular walking, we are in a hurry to immediately shift our weight forward, off the back leg. That is precisely the point in time when it is easy to lose your balance, or when you can disrupt an opponent's balance in tai chi martial arts applications.

You will shift your weight forward onto your left foot, but first visualize and feel that you are a rear-wheel drive vehicle. Sink, and roll your weight down, as if through the ground, and continue to roll it forward onto the front, left leg. Progressively flatten your left foot onto the ground, like a tire rolling on the road. At this point, you will be in a bow-and-arrow stance. Begin to roll your right heel off the ground as you commit your body weight on, and straight down through, your left foot.

You will feel that the ball of your right foot is ready to push off the ground, giving you the momentum to move forward. In regular walking, our dantian is higher. But here, in this tai chi exercise, imagine your dantian sinking. This lowers your center of gravity and allows the *qi* to flow smoothly. Instead of dragging your right foot up to bring it to the forefront, feel how the gentle tucking of your lower back "scoops" it forward. This makes it a whole-body movement instead of a movement externally isolated in the limb.

This whole-body technique is what makes tai chi movement more powerful than regular movement. Repeat the exercise, continuing on doing this as a tai chi walking exercise instead of regular walking.

Half step
You already completed the movement for half step when you scooped your lower back and pelvis to bring the rear leg up while completing the whole step exercise opposite. The only difference is that you stay in a front-weighted empty stance for a moment, and then shift your weight back onto the rear (empty) foot. Remember that when you shift, you must sink your *qi* and movement as if you are rolling it through the ground.

Let's visit half step again here in detail. Begin in a bow-and-arrow stance with the left leg forward. Roll your weight onto the front left leg. Use your pelvis, lower back, and sense of whole-body movement to empty the right foot and draw it in, just a bit behind the left (be sure to not cross the back heel line), as a toe-down empty step. Maintaining upright posture, create the feeling of sinking on your left leg as you

Whole-body movement
The dynamic stances you are learning are what connect the other stances and tai chi postures together. Just as when you are static, when you move, your whole body is involved as one unit in traditional tai chi chuan. From here on, visualize originating your movement from the dantian and concentrically pass that movement through your torso and then to your limbs. If you manifest your tai chi movements in this manner, it is said that you can greatly increase your capacity for *qi*, as well as evolve your levels of coordination and control.

roll your body weight back, through the ground and into your right toes. Roll the toes, sole, and heel of your right foot flat onto the ground, thereby leaving your left foot as an empty step.

From here you can extend your left foot out as an empty step, a kick, a rooster stance, or other stances. Repeat on the other side.

Twist step

The twist step is possibly the most misused and misunderstood step of all tai chi chuan. This footwork pattern can either give you excellent whole-body power or it can damage your knee. It may feel difficult at first, yet it becomes easy rather quickly, if you practice it consistently.

A twist step is predominantly employed to transition an L-stance into a bow-and-arrow stance. A strike usually accompanies the completion of a twist step. For tai chi martial arts, twist step can add tremendous power to a strike.

To understand how this works, get into an L-stance in which your left foot is in front (the stem of the L) and your right foot is in back (the base of the L). Your centerline is in the middle of the stance and your weight is equally distributed.

Keeping your left knee in line with your left toes, begin to shift all your weight onto your left leg, emptying your right foot and allowing it to be mobile. As you shift your weight to the left, flex your right foot so the heel is on the floor and toes point up. Keep your body weight concentrated on your left leg and sink. Relax your chest and drop your dantian. You

Biggest mistake in twist steps

Twist step is one of the most poorly executed steps in tai chi chuan, with most people performing it with too much weight on the twisting leg, which overloads the knee and ankle joints, often buckling in the knee. This is akin to trying to lift up an object while simultaneously loading your body weight onto it. Young or athletic people will not feel it at first, until years of damage accumulate.

If you do it correctly, you should experience no knee pain. Make sure that your front leg stays solid and fixed as you twist step the rear leg. Also note that a twist step is impossible to complete if the stem heel of your L-stance has crossed the back heel line of the base foot. If twist step feels unstable, start with a wider L-stance. If you have knee problems, do this movement from a narrower L-stance.

must truly feel that you are sitting and sinking on the left, weighted leg. If you become the least bit top-heavy, the twist step will feel cumbersome.

Now, inwardly rotate your right thigh, so that your leg and foot also rotate inward, thereby pointing your toes in. Gently tuck your pelvis, flatten your right foot, and drop your body weight straight down into the floor from your perineal area. Sit comfortably into the stance.

You should now find yourself in a bow-and-arrow stance with your centerline facing forward. Twist step is a whole-body movement because it not only turns your foot and leg, but your entire torso as well.

Practice each side again and again until this starts to become increasingly comfortable. If you are right-side dominant, you may find that executing the twist step in your left foot feels more difficult than your right at first; the opposite is true if you are left-side dominant. Therefore, twist steps can show us and help us correct the imbalances in the body. In time, this all becomes very easy.

Lift and rotate

If you cannot rotate your toes in enough on the hooking foot, try this instead: Pick up that foot, rotate your hip, leg, and foot inwardly as one unit, and then set it down on the floor "emptily." Then complete the technique of shifting your weight onto it while releasing weight off the opposite leg. Sometimes this picking up the foot and stepping it in as a hook step is easier then pivoting on the heel to do the job.

To further practice your twist steps, repeatedly do and undo them. From an L-stance, go into a twist step to get into a bow-and arrow stance. Then reverse the entire process to "undo" the twist step to get you back into an L-stance. Repeat on both sides. Take higher and shorter stances if you have joint pain. Always remember to relax and sink with good structure.

Hook Step

The hook step is often used to change direction 180 degrees. The intense inward rotation of the hip may feel odd if you are a beginner, but regular practice of the hook step will increase the flexibility of your hips, making the step easy to do.

In martial application, it is used to trap the opponent with the leg, or to enter an opponent's space to execute a throw with a good shot of torque. For health purposes, it stretches out the external hip rotators, which can benefit the sciatic nerve, lower back, and hips.

To execute a hook step, assume a medium to narrow horse stance. Keeping upright posture, shift all your weight onto your left leg. Keeping your right heel on the floor, flex your foot so the toes are pointing upward.

Pivoting on the right empty heel, turn your hip inwardly as much as possible, so that your right toes point in toward your left foot. As you become more flexible, your toes will point in 90 degrees.

Be sure to keep your pelvis rolled under. Relax on your weighted leg, sinking your weight straight down into your left hip and leg like an elevator descending a shaft. Imagine your weight passing your foot and going into the ground. Then, as if rolling your weight through the ground, transfer your weight into your right foot as you simultaneously empty the left.

If you let go of your left foot and relax, you will notice that your torso wants to turn to the left. Let it. This is the way a hook step helps you change direction. It loads torque and

twist into the hip of your hooked foot. That potential energy turns into kinetic energy as you release all weight off the other leg, thus resulting in a whole-body rotation.

Instead of thinking about hooking your foot inward, think about and feel the rotation coming from your hip. This is what then lets you turn your torso to change direction with great control and ease.

Keep it light

Never keep weight on both feet when a foot is hooked in—look at the strange way it positions and loads your knees. The hook step requires mastery of empty steps. Once you start shifting weight into the hooked foot, you must immediately get it off the other foot.

Twine step

Like the twist step, the twine steps are sophisticated tai chi chuan steps that are so often done incorrectly. Like the hook step, the twine step allows you to change direction rapidly, as well as store energy in your hip. This energy can turn into a powerful kick.

Twine step also goes by the names "cross-legged stance," "sit-stance," and "lotus stance." Like the tiger stance, you can vary how high or deep you take the position, according to your ability. The twine step, in its nature though, is a rather narrow stance. A twine step ties together a back-weighted empty stance with a front-weighted one, while turning the body as much as 90 degrees in the direction that you point the toes of your front foot.

Forward-moving twine step

For a forward-moving twine step, begin with your feet parallel in a rather narrow horse stance. Extend your left foot in front of you as a heel-down back-weighted empty stance. Do not extend your foot too far in front of you.

Sit comfortably on your right leg with your back and head erect and your ears in line with your shoulders. From your left *kua* (hip), outwardly rotate your leg so that your foot turns out as much as 90 degrees. Sink your weight down through your right leg, into the floor, and transfer it into your left leg. Simultaneously allow your torso to turn leftward. Emptily pull your right leg in.

You will find yourself ending in a front-weighted empty stance. Ensure that when you shift your weight onto the left front leg, you keep your posture ramrod straight. Avoid leaning forward or sticking out your buttocks at the end of this move, which could overload your knee joints. Keep your head tucked back and your pelvis rolled under. "Sit" into the stance while relaxing the chest and shoulders. Repeat this exercise on the other side.

Remember: where you point your toes is where your centerline goes

Notice that in moving stances such as the twist step, hook step, and especially in the twine steps, wherever you rotate your leg and toes is where the centerline of your torso winds up facing at the end of the step.

Hip versus *kua*

In tai chi chuan there is much mention of the pelvis and hips. The Chinese concept of "hip" is different than the Western concept. In the West, we think of the hip as the outside edge of the pelvis and thigh. But in the Chinese concept, it refers to the inner areas of the hip—the creases that form the V where the torso meets the thighs. The anatomical name for this is the inguinal crease. The Chinese word for this is the *kua*.

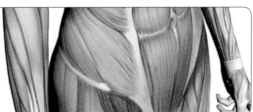

Backward-moving twine step

The backward-moving twine step is not as common as the forward-moving version in tai chi chuan. In essence, it's just a matter of doing a forward-moving twine stance in reverse. It connects a front-weighted empty stance to a back-weighted one. Like the twist step exercise, you must practice doing and undoing the twine step to build control and agility into your nervous system.

To begin a backward-moving twine step, assume a front-weighted empty stance with all your body weight on your left leg. Position the empty toes of your right foot behind and to the outside edge of your left foot. Lightly touch your right toes to the ground

Accomplish this position by a slight outward rotation of your right *kua* and moving your foot into position. It may appear as if you are violating the principle of not crossing the back heel line, but in a moment you will see that this is not the case. Keep your back and head straight.

Sink down into your *kua*, and begin to roll your body weight onto your right toes. Then start letting your torso turn rightward, and finish rolling your right foot onto the ground, carrying your body weight as you immediately empty out your left foot. You wind up in a back-weighted empty stance (on your right foot) with the centerline of your torso facing in the same direction that your right toes are pointing.

Practice this several times, moving forward into a twine step and then moving backward with a twine step. Repeat it on both sides. Try a wider stance and a narrower stance, and explore how other ways of positioning your body either positively or negatively affect the twine stances.

Ramrod straight

To help you achieve perfect posture as you turn, thus preserving your joints and conserving *qi* energy, imagine a steel rod running through you from the top back area of your head, straight through your torso, and out the perineal area, continuing through the ground. Imagine this rod holds you up so that it is impossible to lose your balance. "Feel" how this rod, in perfect alignment with gravity, lets you rotate swiftly. The rod translates through space with you as you move from one point to another, but it always stays perfectly aligned with gravity. This imaginary rod also lets you relax your muscles, since it is holding you up instead of forcing you to overexert to keep upright. Let your body weight sink along this rod and let your head feel as if it is pulled straight up along this invisible rod.

You can get there from here

Whenever there is a spin on one leg in tai chi (mostly seen in Chen Style forms), you can substitute it with a series of narrow twine steps and hook steps to turn your body around. This is especially useful if you have joint pain or a prosthetic leg. Never feel defeated that you can't do it. Simply alter the tai chi posture to make it work for you.

Hand forms

Along with its basic foot positions, tai chi chuan relies on basic hand positions: the palm, hook, and fist. Each position carries the *qi* differently through the hand, and each one has its own martial arts purpose.

The tai chi palm

The tai chi palm is simply the flat of the hand. Most often, you'll extend your wrist to extend your fingers back. At other times, you position your hand so that your fingers are in line with your forearm. Your palm can be energized or relaxed, but never crumple up your fingers. Hold them relatively straight—this helps the *qi* flow through the meridians and helps keep your joints healthy, youthful, and agile.

The belly of the fingers

The original Chen lineage of tai chi chuan talks about the importance of bringing *qi* to the "belly" of the fingers. The belly of the fingers is the first proximal phalange of each finger—the first finger segment closest to the palm.

Tai chi palm exercise

To bring *qi* to the belly of the fingers, we harness the energy normally "trapped" in the shoulder and crook of the neck area of the body, which is a natural energy trap. By making use of this stuck energy, we dredge the *qi* channels and release muscular tension. It also stretches the fascia of the hand and helps to correct joint and soft-tissue imbalances.

Think of the area of your upper back, neck, and shoulder, where you often hold tension. Press your shoulder down slightly, and imagine the energy running down your upper arm and forearm to your hand. Imagine that five pipes branch off from this area and each exit the belly of the fingers. Press down, relax the chest, open the palm, and visualize this trapped energy clearing the obstructions and creating a strong current of energy. Exhale to help you feel this, and then, slightly let up and let your hand relax and soften a little. Make sure that your elbow joint faces down, unlocked. Repeat this exercise several times on each hand. It is an excellent exercise for people with coordination challenges or tremors.

The tai chi hook

The tai chi hook hand formation is used martially to trap, parry, or strike. Its pyramidal structure gives it physical strength, as well as concentrates the *qi* to a smaller area.

Be careful not to lose the *qi* flow when you start to bring the fingers together in this hand form.

To make a proper tai chi hook, bring together all the fingertips of one hand. The tips should be as level with one another as possible. If you have arthritis, amputated fingers, or other prior injury, just approximate the positions as best as you can. The Taoists believe that energy follows thought—so you can still bring your *qi* energy throughout the hand effectively, so long as you have your intent there.

Next, flex your hand downward from the wrist. Practice this hand formation by extending the feeling of stretching trapped energy from your shoulder down to your hand and the belly of the fingers as you did in the tai chi palm exercise. Keep the energy stretching there as you bend your wrist and close your five fingertips together. Make sure that your elbow joint faces down, unlocked.

Plum blossom fingers

While you make a tai chi hook, look at all your fingertips touching—you will notice that their shape resembles a five-petaled flower. This is why some tai chi writings call this hand formation "plum blossom" fingers.

The hand of a fair lady

The Yang tai chi schools sometimes advise you to hold your palm as if it were the palm of a "fair lady." Most people interpret this to mean crumpled-up fingers and collapsed hand structure. Yet, a fair lady is a young woman—her hands would be very flexible, graceful, dexterous, and certainly not crumpled up. To get the proper relaxed hand structure, aim the energy strongly out the belly of the fingers. Pull the palm back hard, and stretch through the palm. Then, simply ease off a little bit to relax the hand. It will remain elastic and dexterous with enough *qi* flow to avoid crumpling up. You can soften the hand even more. If you want to preserve the energy of youthfulness, hold yourself in that manner.

The tai chi fist

The tai chi fist is always held loosely until the moment of real or imagined impact. Impact typically occurs at the final follow-through aspect of the movement. For that instant, imagine that you are busting through some obstacle. Squeeze your fist at the impact, and then immediately relax it again.

To form a strong tai chi fist, roll your fingers in and fold your thumb over the outside second phalange of your first two or three fingers.

The palm of the fist is called the "heart" of the fist. The metacarpals are referred to as the "back" of the fist. The exposed root phalanges are called the "face" of the fist—the striking surface. The curled index finger and thumb base are referred to as the "eye" of the fist, and the curled fifth finger area is named the "heel" of the fist.

Begin with the tai chi palm exercise. As you draw the energy down to the hand, roll your fingers into a fist. You must hold the striking line of the fist in alignment with your wrist, which is straight. Squeeze hard for a quick moment, and then immediately relax the fist. Repeat on the other side.

Neat nails

Ladies and gentlemen, keep your fingernails trimmed if you wish to achieve a proper fist. Women with long nails can use only a loose fist, but should still be sure to wrap the thumb on the outside of the fingers of a fist.

Ready to strike

In tai chi martial arts applications, you relax your striking hand until the moment of impact. At that moment, it is very firm. You then immediately relax again. You should execute most strikes with a whip-like energy. Though your hands should always have a little feeling of *qi* or energy stretching into them, never hold tension in them when practicing tai chi chuan. Holding tension in muscles wastes energy, creates *qi* congestion, and slows down your ability to respond quickly to a situation.

Make tai chi fit you

Tai chi is about self-development. You will come face-to-face with your own obstacles and blockages. Work through them, and make yourself learn to relax through them.

One of the most wonderful things about tai chi is that you can "custom fit" it to your body and needs. If you have pain in your joints, take much higher and narrower stances than shown in the photos. If you desire more improvement in your feelings or moods, then spend more time on the breathing exercises and Yang Style postures. If you need more vitality, work on the Chen Style excerpt (pages 124–143) and Dead Bug (page 153). First work the stances and Yang and Chen sequences to build a foundation. Then peruse the book and engage in a few tai chi exercises that address your specific needs.

Keep it clean

Ninety percent of mastering the movements lies in clean posture and excellent stance work. "Clean" posture means removing the excess "noise" from your structure. The slight hunch, the little excess sway in the lower back, the ears not in line with the shoulders—all these things add up over time. It's like the wheel alignment of a vehicle. Imagine a truck with a bad wheel alignment. At first, it's no big deal, but after time and repeated heavy loads, not only do the wheels wear out,

but the integrity of the axle is affected, too, as well as the brakes, the suspension system . . . and the ride is no longer smooth. Energy is wasted. Repairs are costly and metal fatigue has set in. The inescapable forces of gravity and friction take their toll.

Your body is no different. With repeated movement, misalignment out of gravity causes excess wear and tear, which affect not only the joints and muscles, but also the internal organs. Put everything back in place and you save energy and reduce wear and tear, thus fostering rejuvenation, extra energy reserves, and, as the Taoists say, reversal in the aging process.

Many of us are unaware of how we hold and move our bodies. People new to tai chi are often surprised to learn that all they need to do to eliminate joint pain is to position their posture differently. They didn't realize that they were holding their body and moving it in ways that facilitated pain and injury instead of strength and healing. They didn't realize how weak their stabilizer muscles were, and that a few weeks of slow, conscientious tai chi practice could remedy in only a few months problems that took decades to develop. Balance improves, energy increases, and healing begins. With a properly aligned body comes properly aligned nerves and organs. This results better moods and higher energy—and that leads to a better quality of life.

How to use this book

This book provides you with a very basic introduction to tai chi chuan. The closer you pay attention to building the basics, however, the better your development and understanding will become.

You'll first begin with the fundamentals—the stances and steps that will move you through the tai chi forms (pages 26–39). Like a house, tai chi is built from the foundation up. At its base is the footwork. No matter how flowing your movements look or how slowly and gracefully you sway about through space, you will not get optimum benefits if your stances are off. Knowing the stances and steps will also make it easier for you to understand tai chi movements. Once you can move through a stance or step with great ease, you have mastered it. Thereafter, you can easily master any tai chi posture that utilizes that stance.

Once you have familiarized yourself with the footwork, move on to postures. Section 1 takes you through the Yang 24 Short Form (pages 46–123), an excellent introduction to the essential elements of tai chi. By learning the Yang 24 Short Form, you will have enough tai chi knowledge to easily fit into various tai chi classes, workshops, and conventions. It also gives you a sense of confidence and completion.

Section 2 offers you a taste of the classic Chen Style with a series of movements excerpted from the form known as Xin Jia Pao Chui, or "New Frame Cannon Fist."

For the postures featured in both sections 1 and 2, you'll find a short introduction to the posture, step-by-step instructions explaining how to do it, some tips on correct form and what to avoid, and anatomical illustrations that show you just what muscles you are engaging. An at-a-glance sidebar gives you a fast visual references of the posture's target muscles, its level of difficulty, its benefits, and any cautions that may apply and what solution will work to overcome them. Also included is the key footwork—these are the steps and stances you need to know to tackle the posture. Work through the steps and stances, and then try the postures that require the steps you've mastered.

Don't rush through the postures; pick one or two to try at a time, and work on mastering them before you move on. As you learn individual postures, try putting them together. When you have mastered all the postures in a section, move through all of them in a smooth flowing sequence.

Learn to visualize

The step-by-step instructions will often ask you to visualize a certain image as you practice a posture, such as imagining that you are holding a large lightweight sphere or balloon between your hands. Learn to use these visualization cues to help you achieve the best possible positioning.

Finding time to practice

Tai chi masters have traditionally recommended an hour of practice per day. Along with tai chi form work, this hour may also include special exercises, breath work, and meditation. You can also work just on a small section of the form over and over again, until you know it well. The best answer is contained within you. Your inner self knows what it needs—it's up to you to start to listen to it.

The clock face

To help you understand directions and where to face, imagine your space as an analog clock face that stays fixed as you move. Your centerline points to the various numbers of the clock where the little hour hand would face. For example, you start your tai chi at 12:00. That means behind you is 6:00, to your right is 3:00, and to your left is 9:00. If you face between 1:00 and 2:00, it's like the little hour hand being in between them at 1:30.

If you are short on time, exercise your creativity by seeking to employ tai chi principles in your day-to-day movements. Remember that tai chi is something you bring into your life. If you always keep it segregated from daily life, it will keep you segregated from all its benefits. Your goal is to make it an effortless practice and way of moving, thinking, feeling, and being. Always look for evidence and opportunities of it flowing into your body, mind, and life. Then you don't have to "do it"; instead, the tai chi "does you."

The tai chi tightrope

Tai chi requires one thing from you: the desire to develop your patience and diligence. If you are not willing to pay this price, you cannot reap the rewards. Tai chi is not a magic bullet. In the case of any pain or problem, of course, first check with your doctor, and then ask for clearance to engage in a practice of tai chi.

Next, be very logical about your practice. If you overdo it and hurt, next time, scale back on the intensity and watch the result. Increase the intensity as your energy rises and your body becomes increasingly conditioned. It is like commencing a practice of weight-lifting. Add more and more, little by little, and watch the result.

Underdoing your practice will lead to scanty or no results. Overdoing it will lead to pain or setbacks. Don't push yourself too hard, but don't be indolent either. And if you stop for a while, don't be discouraged or feel guilty. Forgive yourself and move on. Applaud yourself for the efforts and things you can do and did do, and refuse to berate yourself what you can't do or didn't do.

Keep a tai chi journal to record a minimum of five things you've seen improve over time, or five things you worked on to improve yourself with tai chi. Do not write a single negative thing. As the good thoughts collect, you will experience improvements in your quality of life.

Full-body anatomy

Front view
Annotation Key
* indicates deep muscles

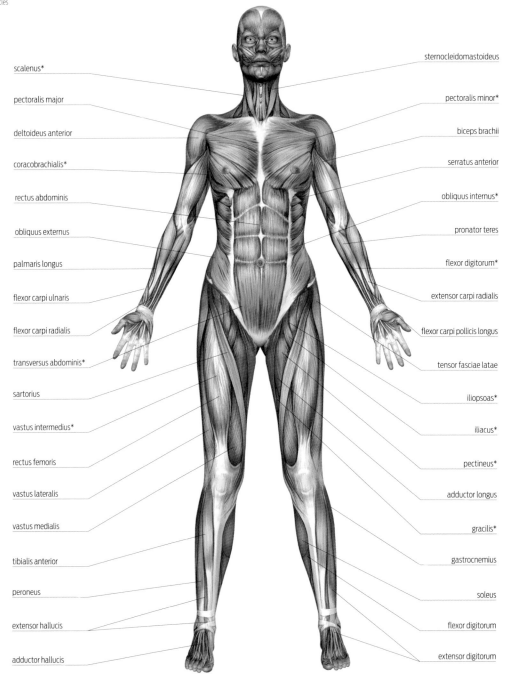

scalenus*

pectoralis major

deltoideus anterior

coracobrachialis*

rectus abdominis

obliquus externus

palmaris longus

flexor carpi ulnaris

flexor carpi radialis

transversus abdominis*

sartorius

vastus intermedius*

rectus femoris

vastus lateralis

vastus medialis

tibialis anterior

peroneus

extensor hallucis

adductor hallucis

sternocleidomastoideus

pectoralis minor*

biceps brachii

serratus anterior

obliquus internus*

pronator teres

flexor digitorum*

extensor carpi radialis

flexor carpi pollicis longus

tensor fasciae latae

iliopsoas*

iliacus*

pectineus*

adductor longus

gracilis*

gastrocnemius

soleus

flexor digitorum

extensor digitorum

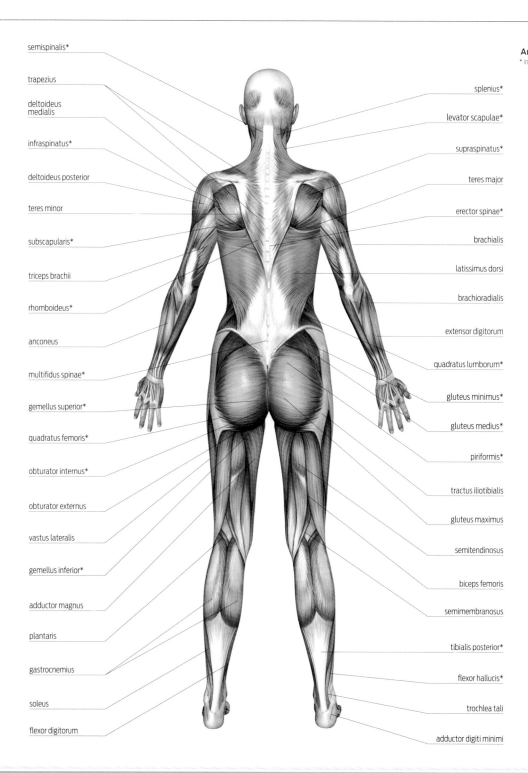

semispinalis*

trapezius

deltoideus
medialis

infraspinatus*

deltoideus posterior

teres minor

subscapularis*

triceps brachii

rhomboideus*

anconeus

multifidus spinae*

gemellus superior*

quadratus femoris*

obturator internus*

obturator externus

vastus lateralis

gemellus inferior*

adductor magnus

plantaris

gastrocnemius

soleus

flexor digitorum

splenius*

levator scapulae*

supraspinatus*

teres major

erector spinae*

brachialis

latissimus dorsi

brachioradialis

extensor digitorum

quadratus lumborum*

gluteus minimus*

gluteus medius*

piriformis*

tractus iliotibialis

gluteus maximus

semitendinosus

biceps femoris

semimembranosus

tibialis posterior*

flexor hallucis*

trochlea tali

adductor digiti minimi

Contents

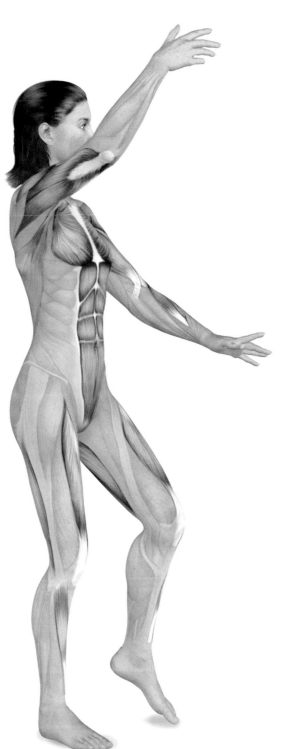

The following pages will take you through the Yang 24 Short Form, one of the most popular tai chi forms in the world today. As its name suggests, this form is composed of 24 postures excerpted from the Traditional Yang Long Form, which contains more than 100 tai chi chuan postures.

The Yang 24 Short Form tai chi chuan has enough variation between the left and right sides of the body to give you a balanced workout. It uses high postures, low postures, wide postures, and narrow postures, with a nice balance of static stancework and dynamic stancework. Start by studying one posture a week.

The Yang 24 Short Form is very rhythmic and patient in nature. If you have a hard time calming down, precede your practice with 5 to 8 minutes of the breathing methods covered on pages 146–147.

If you prefer to practice tai chi at night, try using this form for your tai chi practice. Turn the lights down low, and set a soothing, peaceful environment by playing calming music. It is easy to practice this form in a loose pair of pajamas. Along with calming you, it may help your digestion and ease insomnia.

Yang style

Opening Posture

At the break of dawn, the earth turns from the darkness of night to the birth of a new day. So too does the Opening Posture welcome you into the mind-set of tai chi chuan. Before commencing movement, stand silently, preparing yourself for unity of mind and body. When you feel this silent connection, let that be the moment you usher in the movement of tai chi chuan. This is the traditional way to use Opening Posture.

1 Facing 12 o'clock, stand straight with your arms at your sides. Position your feet close together, parallel, in a narrow horse stance. Imagine there are small spheres under your armpits so that your arms are not pressed against your body. Keep your fingers open and lightly stretched—relaxed, but not curled up. Press the energy from your shoulders down to your fingers.

2 Shift your weight to your right foot, and step out your left foot to slightly widen your horse stance, so that your feet are parallel and shoulder-width apart.

3 Sink your weight onto both feet equally. Lower your body as you let your arms rise in front of you to shoulder height, as if floating upward effortlessly. Keep your palms face down.

Correct form
- Keep as straight as an elevator descending an elevator shaft while lowering yourself with your buttocks tucked.

Avoid
- Squatting too low—go only far as is comfortable to your knees while maintaining an upright posture.

4 Relax your elbows downward so that your arms bend slightly. Continue to lower your body by bending your knees and ankles and sinking into your *kua*. Leave your arms as if they were floating on the surface of water while your body continues to sink.

5 Squat only as low as you can maintain erect posture, and then begin to rise. Like a lever, this movement lowers your arms and pushes your palms down to waist level.

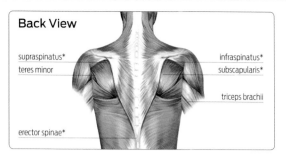

Back View

supraspinatus*
teres minor

infraspinatus*
subscapularis*

triceps brachii

erector spinae*

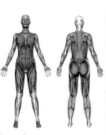

Level
· All levels

Footwork
· Horse stance

Benefits
· Strengthens legs
· Releases tension
  from body

Caution
· Safe for most

deltoideus anterior

coracobrachialis

biceps brachii

rectus abdominis

vastus intermedius*

rectus femoris

vastus lateralis

vastus medialis

gastrocnemius

Back View

tractus iliotibialis

semitendinosus

biceps femoris

semimembranosus

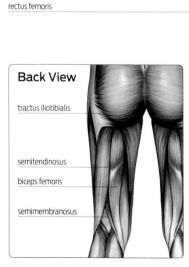

Annotation Key
* indicates deep muscles

Wild Horse Parts Mane Left

Spiritual aesthetics are deeply valued in the East. As such, tai chi often employs poetic imagery in the names of its postures. For this one, picture a scene of wild horses running freely on the open plains. The wind tousles their manes to and fro as they gracefully gallop into the distance. Wild Horse Parts Mane shows the grace, power, and control of the mustang, as the arms switch positions, mimicking a mane parting side-to-side in the wind.

1 Shift your weight to your right foot and slightly twist your body to the left as you simultaneously bring your left foot in near your right as an empty step. Imagine that you are holding a large sphere between your hands. Your right hand is above and your left hand below with palms facing each other. Your right hand is at the height of your right shoulder with elbow relaxed slightly downward.

2 Step out your left heel as an empty step, with toes pointing to 9 o'clock. As you begin to flatten your left foot onto the floor, face your torso to 9 o'clock, which will put you in an L-stance.

3 Shift forward into a bow-and-arrow stance using a twist step. Separate your hands as if they were a seesaw. Your left arm extends outward and upward in front of you at eye level, arm vertical, fingers up, and palm facing you. Your right palm pushes down near your hip.

4 As you shift forward into the bow-and-arrow stance, twist step on your right heel by turning in at the *kua* so that your right toes point to approximately 10 o'clock. Flatten your right foot on the floor and sink by relaxing downward.

Correct form
· Keep buttocks tucked, and ensure a clear back heel line when you step out into the L-stance.
· Use clearly defined twist and twine steps.

Avoid
· Twisting your body at the knees: instead, twist from the *kua*.

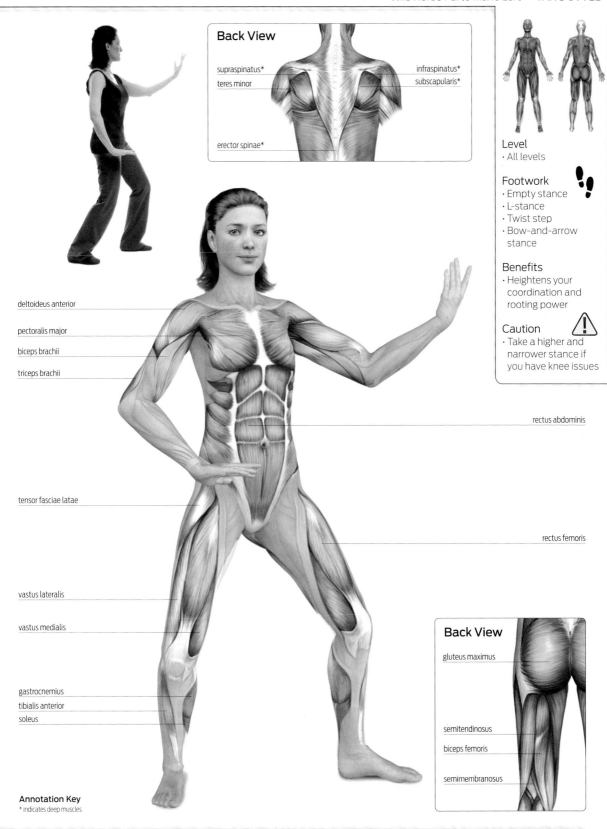

Back View

supraspinatus*
teres minor

infraspinatus*
subscapularis*

erector spinae*

Level
· All levels

Footwork
· Empty stance
· L-stance
· Twist step
· Bow-and-arrow stance

Benefits
· Heightens your coordination and rooting power

Caution
· Take a higher and narrower stance if you have knee issues

deltoideus anterior

pectoralis major

biceps brachii

triceps brachii

rectus abdominis

tensor fasciae latae

rectus femoris

vastus lateralis

vastus medialis

gastrocnemius
tibialis anterior
soleus

Back View

gluteus maximus

semitendinosus

biceps femoris

semimembranosus

Annotation Key
* indicates deep muscles

Wild Horse Parts Mane Right

Wild Horse Parts Mane is also referred to as Mustang Ruffles Mane—it simply depends on the translator. You will repeat this posture three times, so it is an excellent study in balancing the left and right sides of the brain and body. Take time to work these moves—with dedicated practice you will see greater grace and coordination.

1 Sink back onto your right leg, but keep your left heel on the floor with toes pointing upward in a back-weighted empty stance. Turn your entire body leftward so that your left toes point toward 6 o'clock via outward rotation of your left *kua*.

2 Go into a forward-moving twine step by shifting all your weight onto your left foot, flattening it on the floor. At the same time rotate your left palm down, and bring your right hand underneath (palm up), near your abdomen, as if holding a sphere.

3 Bring your right foot next to your left foot as an empty step with heel up, toes touching the floor.

4 Step your right leg forward as an empty step, touching the heel down first. As you shift your weight forward onto your right foot, turn your centerline to face 9 o'clock by using a twist step in your left foot. At the same time, seesaw your arms: your right arm extends out and up in front of you at eye level, fingers pointing up, elbow down, while your left hand pushes down to your left hip with palm face down.

5 Repeat Wild Horse Parts Mane Left, ending in a bow-and-arrow stance.

Correct form
· Keep buttocks tucked, and ensure a clear back heel line when you step out into the L-stance.
· Use clearly defined twist and twine steps.

Avoid
· Twisting your body at the knees: instead, twist from the *kua*.

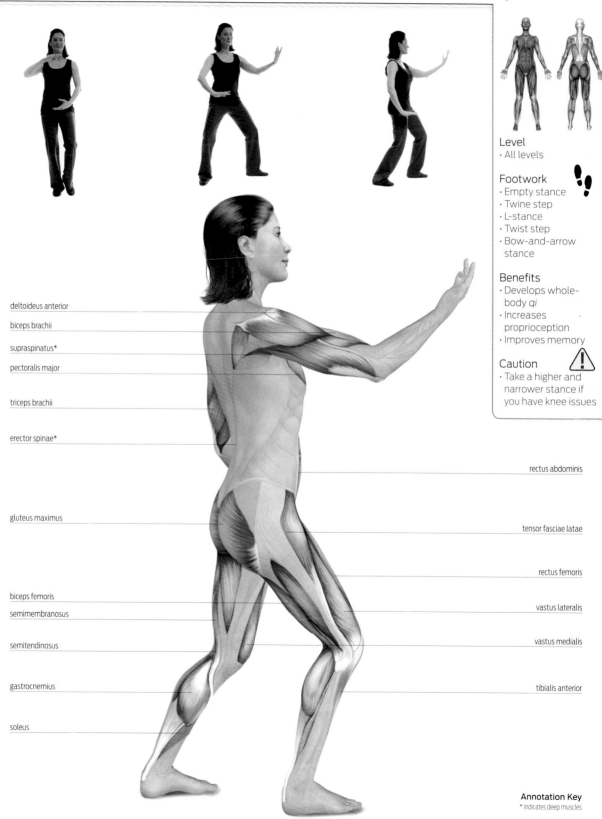

Level
· All levels

Footwork
· Empty stance
· Twine step
· L-stance
· Twist step
· Bow-and-arrow stance

Benefits
· Develops whole-body *qi*
· Increases proprioception
· Improves memory

Caution ⚠
· Take a higher and narrower stance if you have knee issues

deltoideus anterior

biceps brachii

supraspinatus*

pectoralis major

triceps brachii

erector spinae*

gluteus maximus

biceps femoris

semimembranosus

semitendinosus

gastrocnemius

soleus

rectus abdominis

tensor fasciae latae

rectus femoris

vastus lateralis

vastus medialis

tibialis anterior

Annotation Key
* indicates deep muscles

White Crane Spreads Wings

The crane is valued in China as a symbol of nobility, wisdom, patience, and longevity, and within the White Crane Spreads Wings posture, you will find grace, power, and silence. As you move through it, find relaxation, yet spiritual alertness. Even though you are standing, be sure to sink the energy down as well.

1 Turn your torso very slightly to your left. Rotate your left palm to face your right, and then slightly push your left palm down, gently bending your left elbow. Simultaneously extend your right arm forward and begin to sweep it in a curve across your body. Pull your right foot in emptily.

2 Step your right foot out sideways into a horse stance, still facing 9 o'clock. As your weight sinks equally to both feet, your palms face each other.

3 Continue to sweep your right arm up in front of your body, past your left elbow, toward your left shoulder. Begin to sink onto your right leg as you rotate your right palm outward and push it out across your body at forehead level, while your left hand finishes pushing out and down to your left hip.

4 Touch your left foot down as an empty step with your heel up and the ball of your foot on the floor. All your weight is on your right leg.

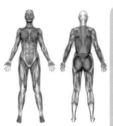

Correct form
· Imagine you are sitting on a high stool.

Avoid
· Leaning during this posture.
· Holding your *qi* and center of gravity too high—relax and drain your chest area

Back View

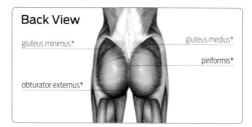

gluteus minimus*

gluteus medius*

piriformis*

obturator externus*

Level
· All levels

Footwork
· Empty stance

Benefits
· Improves bodily control and balance
· Heightens awareness

Caution
· Keep your right arm low if you have shoulder issues

Annotation Key
* indicates deep muscles

triceps brachii

deltoideus medialis

deltoideus posterior

pectoralis major

latissimus dorsi

serratus anterior

gluteus maximus

tensor fasciae latae

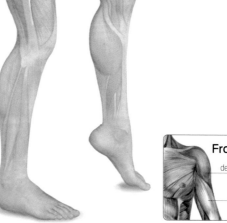

Front View

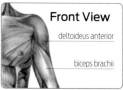

deltoideus anterior

biceps brachii

Brush Knee and Twist Step Left

Tai chi is only a few stances connected together, with the myriad differences occurring in the arm positions. Brush Knee and Twist Step is a prime example—if you remove the arms from the movement, you'll notice that it is exactly the same footwork as Wild Horse Parts Mane. Think carefully about your arm positioning throughout the posture.

1 Turn your torso slightly to the right from the *kua*, and rotate your arms so that your palms face each other. Like the pendulum of a grandfather clock, swing your arms down and back (at your right side), as your left arm sweeps in front of your body to the right side of your chest and your right arm extends back slightly behind you, at shoulder level. Keep your weight on your right leg.

2 Step out your left heel to 9 o'clock. As you begin to shift your weight forward, push your right palm past your right ear, elbow down. Continue to shift your weight forward into a bow-and-arrow stance while pushing your right palm forward and brushing your left hand outwardly above your left knee and then down to your left hip (pointing palm down).

3 Gently twist-step your right foot to complete the bow-and-arrow stance.

Correct form
· Use clearly defined twist and twine steps.

Avoid
· Twisting your body at the knees: rotate from the *kua*.

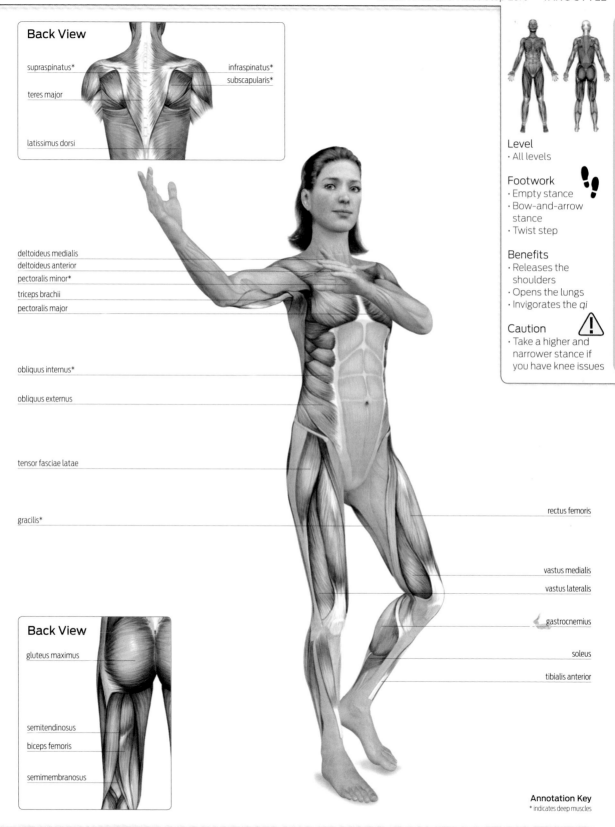

Back View

supraspinatus*

infraspinatus*

subscapularis*

teres major

latissimus dorsi

Level
· All levels

Footwork
· Empty stance
· Bow-and-arrow
  stance
· Twist step

Benefits
· Releases the
  shoulders
· Opens the lungs
· Invigorates the *qi*

Caution
· Take a higher and
  narrower stance if
  you have knee issues

deltoideus medialis
deltoideus anterior
pectoralis minor*
triceps brachii
pectoralis major

obliquus internus*

obliquus externus

tensor fasciae latae

gracilis*

rectus femoris

vastus medialis

vastus lateralis

gastrocnemius

soleus

tibialis anterior

Back View

gluteus maximus

semitendinosus

biceps femoris

semimembranosus

Annotation Key
* indicates deep muscles

Brush Knee and Twist Step Right

Brush Knee and Twist Step is another posture that you repeat during the Yang 24 Short Form. If you know one side, you can easily figure out the other side. Once your brain learns how to compare one side to the other, all your movements become easier. Take time on the side that is the greater challenge for you, until you feel it get easier.

1 Moving your body as a whole unit, sink back onto your right leg, while keeping your left heel on floor with your toes pointing upward in a back-weighted empty stance.

2 Turn your entire body leftward so that your left toes point to 6 o'clock via outward rotation of your left *kua*. At the same time, rotate your arms so that your palms face each other. Like the pendulum of a grandfather clock, swing your arms down and back (at your left side), as your right arm sweeps in front of your body to the left side of your chest and your left arm extends back a bit behind you, at shoulder level. Keep your weight on your right leg.

3 Go into a forward-moving twine step by shifting all your weight onto your left foot, flattening it on the floor. Pull your right foot in emptily. You should now face 6 o'clock.

4 Step out your right heel to 9 o'clock. As you begin to shift your weight forward, push your left palm past your left ear, elbow down. Continue to shift your weight forward into a bow-and-arrow stance while pushing your left palm forward and brushing your right hand outwardly above your right knee and then down to your right hip (pointing palm down).

5 Gently twist step your left foot to complete the bow-and-arrow stance.

6 Repeat Brush and Twist Step Left to end in the bow-and-arrow stance

Correct form

· Use clearly defined twist and twine steps.
· As you tuck your pelvis, keep your head in proper posture by keeping your ears in line with your shoulders.

Avoid

· Twisting your body at the knees: instead, twist from the *kua*.
· Hunching over to brush your knee by touching it—just brush above it while keeping your posture erect.

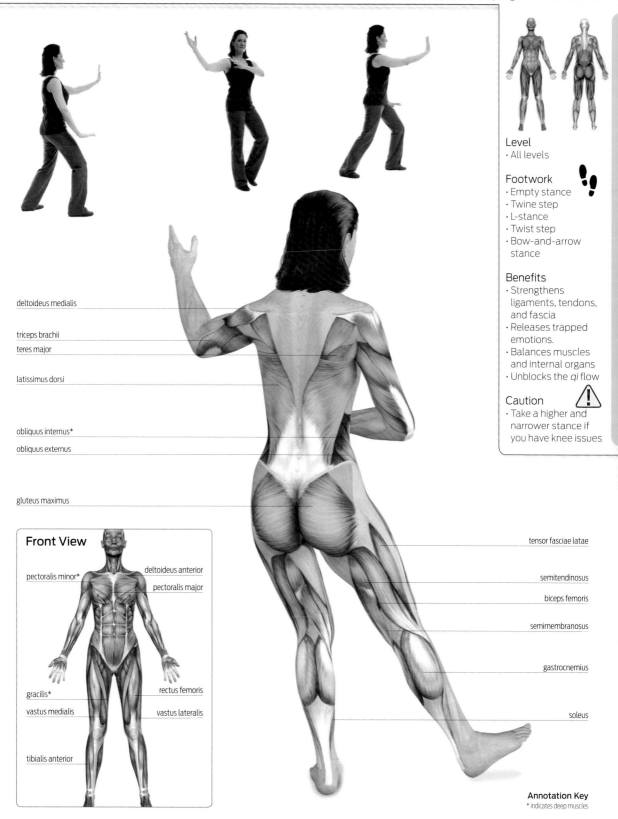

Level
· All levels

Footwork
· Empty stance
· Twine step
· L-stance
· Twist step
· Bow-and-arrow stance

Benefits
· Strengthens ligaments, tendons, and fascia
· Releases trapped emotions.
· Balances muscles and internal organs
· Unblocks the *qi* flow

Caution
· Take a higher and narrower stance if you have knee issues

deltoideus medialis

triceps brachii

teres major

latissimus dorsi

obliquus internus*

obliquus externus

gluteus maximus

tensor fasciae latae

semitendinosus

biceps femoris

semimembranosus

gastrocnemius

soleus

Front View

pectoralis minor*

deltoideus anterior

pectoralis major

gracilis*

rectus femoris

vastus medialis

vastus lateralis

tibialis anterior

Annotation Key
* indicates deep muscles

Playing Pipa

The pipa is a classical Chinese string instrument, akin to the European lute or mandolin. This tai chi posture is sometimes called "Playing Guitar," but unlike a guitar, the pipa is held in a nearly upright position. Remember that tai chi is a whole-body movement, so just like a virtuoso musician, use your entire body and entire spirit to play this tai chi pipa.

1 Half step your right foot forward closely so that the inside of your right heel almost touches the back of your left heel. As you shift your weight back onto your right foot, raise up your right arm, leading with your wrist, bending it so that the thumb's base points up and your palm faces left.

2 Emptily step your left leg forward onto your heel with your toes up and all your weight on your right foot. At same time, turn your torso slightly to the right as you begin to raise your left arm. Your palms face each other.

3 Rotate your torso forward to 9 o'clock while momentarily squeezing your shoulders inward. While squeezing, lower your right hand as if strumming a lute while your left hand finishes rising to shoulder height. Both your palms face inward, with your left hand slightly higher than your right.

4 Keep your elbows slightly bent and facing down. Your right palm finishes at height of your left elbow. Situate the fingers of your right hand parallel with your left forearm. Be sure your left hand is in line with your torso's centerline. At end of this posture, release the "squeeze," thereby relaxing your chest and shoulders.

Correct form
· Extend your arms in front of you with your
  elbows relaxed.

Avoid
· Leaning either too far forward or backwards.
· Crumpling up your arms; keep fingers straight
  but relaxed.

Level
· All levels

Footwork
· Half step
· Empty stance

Benefits
· Releases tension
  from heart and lungs
· Builds coordination

Caution
· Instead of the heel,
  touch toes down as
  an empty stance if
  you have heel spurs

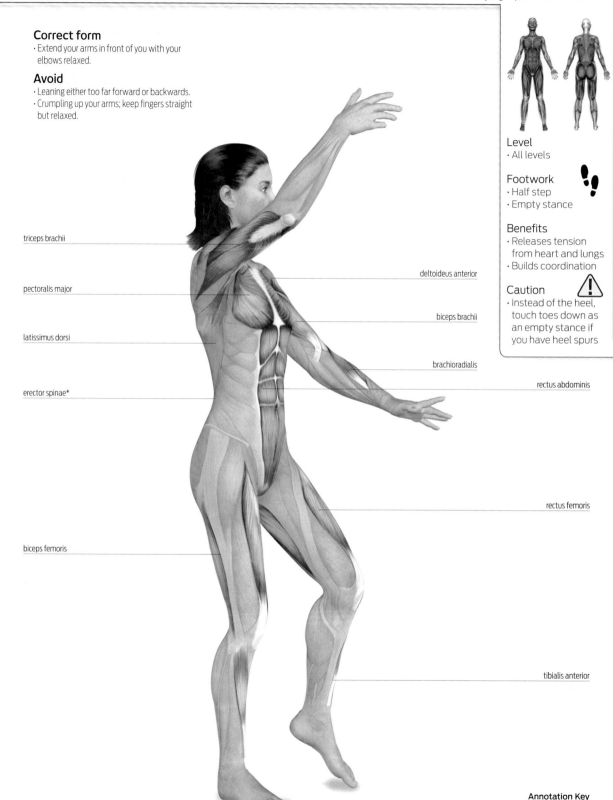

triceps brachii

pectoralis major

latissimus dorsi

erector spinae*

biceps femoris

deltoideus anterior

biceps brachii

brachioradialis

rectus abdominis

rectus femoris

tibialis anterior

Annotation Key
* indicates deep muscles

Repulse Monkey Right

You move backwards for the Repulse Monkey posture, repeating it a total of four times, alternating between the right and left sides. You face 9 o'clock at the end of each Repulse Monkey segment, with the toes of your front empty leg facing 9 o'clock at the end of each move. Exercise physiologists recommend that walkers and runners move backward, as well as forward, during their workouts. Moving backward engages the neuromuscular connections in a different way and provides a well-rounded exercise regimen.

1 Rotate your torso slightly to the right while sweeping your right arm down to your side, turning your right palm upward and your left downward. Continue to extend your right arm behind you with the elbow gently bent. Retract your left leg and arm. Step your left leg behind you and slightly outward.

2 Orient your torso forward to face 9 o'clock as you slowly push your right palm forward and pull your left hand to your hip with the palm up. Simultaneously shift all your weight back onto your left leg.

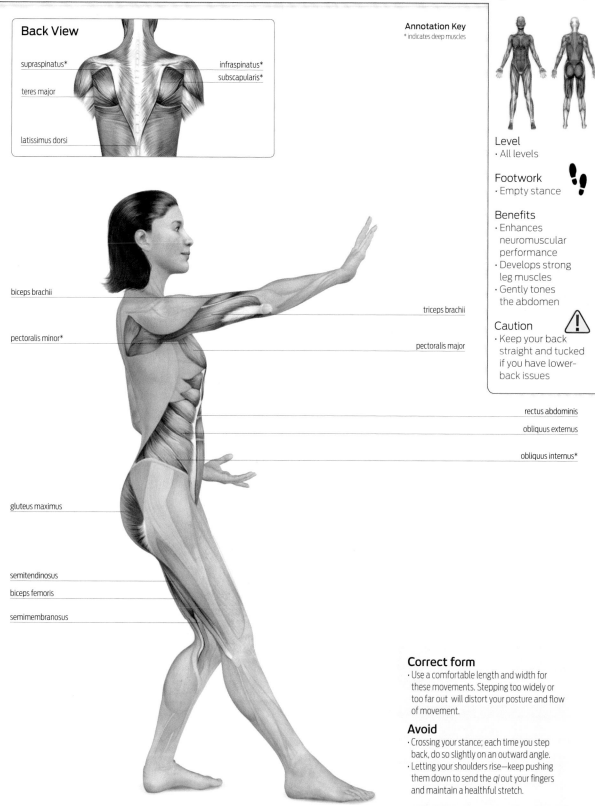

Back View

supraspinatus*

infraspinatus*
subscapularis*

teres major

latissimus dorsi

Annotation Key
* indicates deep muscles

Level
· All levels

Footwork
· Empty stance

Benefits
· Enhances
  neuromuscular
  performance
· Develops strong
  leg muscles
· Gently tones
  the abdomen

Caution
· Keep your back
  straight and tucked
  if you have lower-
  back issues

biceps brachii

triceps brachii

pectoralis minor*

pectoralis major

rectus abdominis

obliquus externus

obliquus internus*

gluteus maximus

semitendinosus

biceps femoris

semimembranosus

Correct form
· Use a comfortable length and width for
  these movements. Stepping too widely or
  too far out will distort your posture and flow
  of movement.

Avoid
· Crossing your stance; each time you step
  back, do so slightly on an outward angle.
· Letting your shoulders rise—keep pushing
  them down to send the *qi* out your fingers
  and maintain a healthful stretch.

Repulse Monkey Left

Ancient Taoist and Buddhist stories refer to the uncultivated mind as the "monkey mind." Today's fast-paced, immediate-gratification values are said to build up the monkey mind rather than mature, spiritual wisdom. Tai chi's mindful and meditative motions are the perfect antidote. Let the pushing hand of these movements symbolize your willpower to fend off the chaotic "monkey energy" of the world. Let the retreating motion remind you of your personal boundaries and a return to the silent wisdom within.

1 Rotate your torso slightly to the left while sweeping your left arm down, behind, and up. Turn your right palm up, and retract your right leg and arm.

2 Step your right leg behind you and slightly outward, and then orient your torso forward as you slowly push your left palm forward while dropping your elbow and pulling your right hand, palm up, to your hip. Simultaneously shift all your weight back onto your right leg.

3 Rotate your torso slightly to the right, and repeat Repulse Monkey Right.

4 Rotate your torso slightly to the left, and repeat Repulse Monkey Left to end facing 9 o'clock.

Correct form
· Gently retract your front leg to shorten the length of your stance to remove strain from your back knee.

Avoid
· Placing your front leg too far forward, which will make you stoop over.

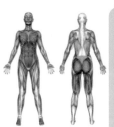

Level
· All levels

Footwork
· Empty stance

Benefits
· Floors your energy
· Strengthens core, back, and legs
· Tones arms

Caution
· Keep your back straight and tucked if you have lower-back issues

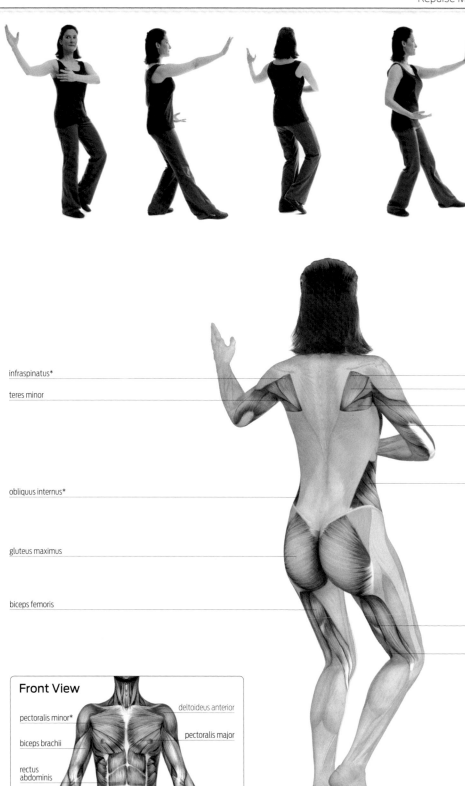

infraspinatus*

teres minor

suprapinatus

subscapularis*

teres major

triceps brachii

obliquus externus

obliquus internus*

gluteus maximus

biceps femoris

semitendinosus

semimembranosus

Front View

pectoralis minor*

deltoideus anterior

biceps brachii

pectoralis major

rectus
abdominis

Annotation Key
* indicates deep muscles

Grasp Sparrow's Tail: Ward Off Left

Grasp Sparrow's Tail is a popular sequence from traditional Yang Style tai chi chuan. Composed of four fundamental postures, Ward Off, Roll Back, Press, and Push, it calls for harmonious movements of the legs, body, and hands. Grasp Sparrow's Tail always begins with Ward Off, which is used martially to root a force and can also be used as a strike.

1 Facing 9 o'clock, place all your weight on your right foot, retracting your left foot next to it as an empty step. At the same time, place your right arm above and your left arm below, rounded out, with palms facing each other as if holding a very large, lightweight sphere. Make sure your shoulders and elbows are relaxed downward. Your hands should be in line with the centerline of your torso, and your torso should be slightly rotated to the right.

2 Begin to step out your left heel, toes pointing to 9 o'clock. Slowly shift your weight onto your left foot to get into a bow-and-arrow stance. At the same time, let your arms "see-saw" apart, with your right hand pulling to your right hip, palm facing the floor, and your left arm extending in front of you, arm held horizontally, palm facing you. As you do this, your torso rotates a little to the left, ending centered to 9 o'clock.

Correct form
· Sink your pelvis, and imagine wrapping your left arm around a large, lightweight sphere.
· Keep your shoulders down and your head pulled straight.
· Slant your left elbow slightly downward.
· Firmly plant your feet.

Avoid
· Stepping out too far—keep your step the length of a normal large walking stride.
· Overextending or trying to reach out; instead, keep your arms within a comfortable range and "sit" into the posture.

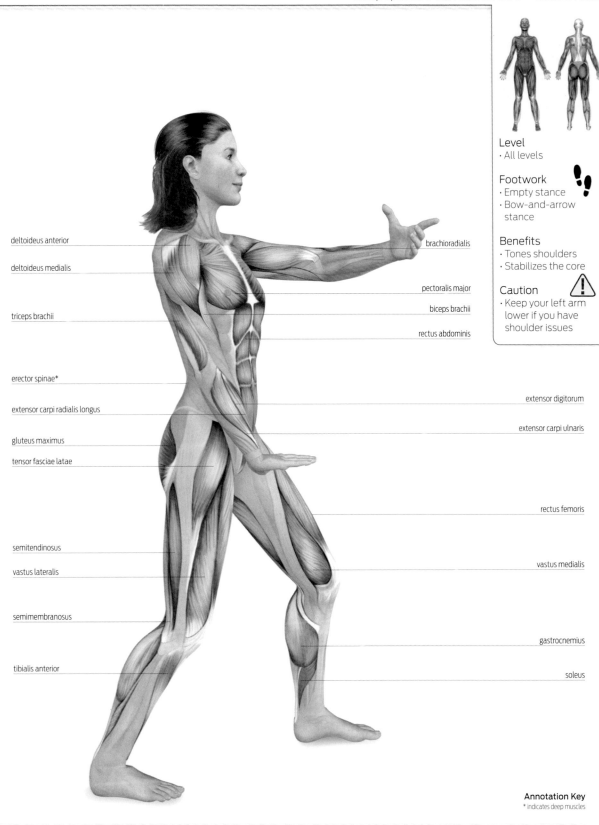

Level
· All levels

Footwork
· Empty stance
· Bow-and-arrow
  stance

Benefits
· Tones shoulders
· Stabilizes the core

Caution
· Keep your left arm
  lower if you have
  shoulder issues

deltoideus anterior

deltoideus medialis

triceps brachii

erector spinae*

extensor carpi radialis longus

gluteus maximus

tensor fasciae latae

semitendinosus

vastus lateralis

semimembranosus

tibialis anterior

brachioradialis

pectoralis major

biceps brachii

rectus abdominis

extensor digitorum

extensor carpi ulnaris

rectus femoris

vastus medialis

gastrocnemius

soleus

Annotation Key
* indicates deep muscles

Grasp Sparrow's Tail: Roll Back Left

The complete opposite of Ward Off, which developed as a move to fend off an attacker, Roll Back is a very yielding energy. Enjoy the interplay between these two different, yet harmonious energies. And although Roll Back is yielding, it is not weak. It is like water—think of the current of a river that has power, yet can easily curve around rocks and other obstacles.

1 From Ward Off, turn your torso slightly to the right as you rotate your arm so that your palms face each other. Imagine that between your palms there is a very large, lightweight sphere.

2 Slowly shift your weight onto your back leg as your arms sweep down, and then slightly upward. Your left hand will be at the height of your right armpit, and your right arm will be slightly extended out and back. Keep your elbows down your pelvis tucked, and your right knee facing outward.

Correct form
· To avoid knee strain, keep your right knee facing out, tuck, and don't overdo it. Use straddle stretches to loosen your adductors.
· Tuck your pelvis as you finish this move to avoid pinching your lower back.

Avoid
· Sticking out your buttocks or leaning forward.
· Sweeping your arms too far back—this pulls too much on the spine.
· Overly rotating your body to the right.

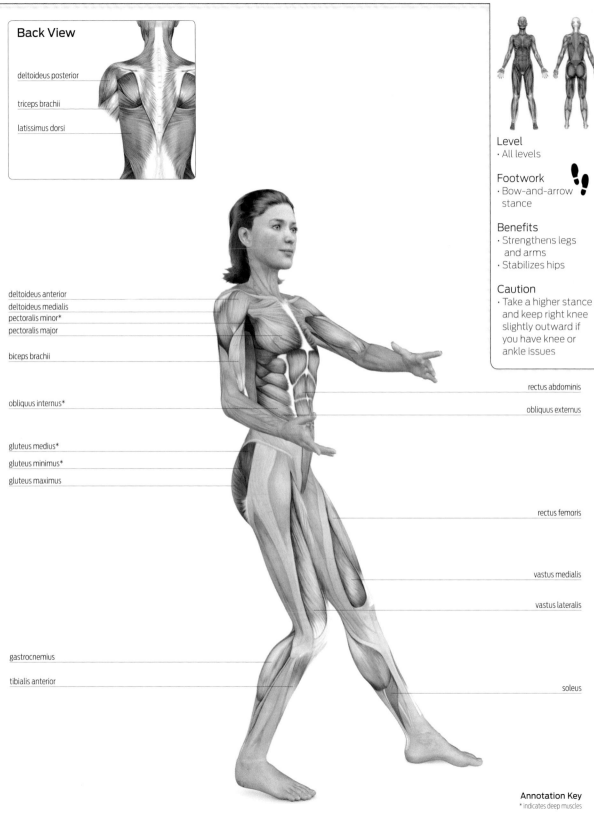

Back View

deltoideus posterior

triceps brachii

latissimus dorsi

Level
· All levels

Footwork
· Bow-and-arrow
  stance

Benefits
· Strengthens legs
  and arms
· Stabilizes hips

Caution
· Take a higher stance
  and keep right knee
  slightly outward if
  you have knee or
  ankle issues

deltoideus anterior
deltoideus medialis
pectoralis minor*
pectoralis major

biceps brachii

obliquus internus*

gluteus medius*

gluteus minimus*

gluteus maximus

gastrocnemius

tibialis anterior

rectus abdominis

obliquus externus

rectus femoris

vastus medialis

vastus lateralis

soleus

Annotation Key
* indicates deep muscles

Grasp Sparrow's Tail: Press Left

Press is an interesting mix of vertical and horizontal forces traveling through your arms and rooted from your feet. Align your posture so that you feel the connection of the earth traveling in a line from your feet, through your spine and shoulders, and out your arms and hands.

1 From Roll Back, start to shift forward, beginning to rotate your torso to again face 9 o'clock.

2 When your weight is equally distributed between both legs, bring the heels of your hand and wrist areas together to touch each other, forming a cross shape with your left hand on the outside and your right hand on the inside. The fingers of your left hand should be horizontal and the right fingers vertical, and your left arm will be more horizontal.

3 As you continue to shift forward onto your left leg, your torso continues to rotate to face 9 o'clock. At the end of the move, your hands should be in line with the centerline of your body, at chest level.

Correct form
· Imagine that there is a large, lightweight sphere between your arms.
· Sit comfortably into the posture.

Avoid
· Overextending; keep the rounded sphere shape between your arms and keep your shoulders and elbows relaxed downward.

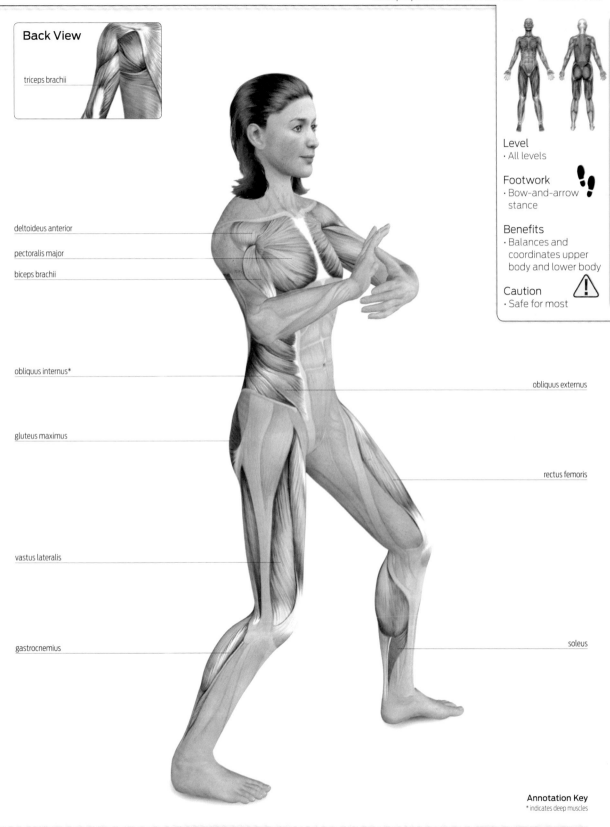

Back View

triceps brachii

deltoideus anterior

pectoralis major

biceps brachii

obliquus internus*

obliquus externus

gluteus maximus

rectus femoris

vastus lateralis

gastrocnemius

soleus

Level
· All levels

Footwork
· Bow-and-arrow
  stance

Benefits
· Balances and
  coordinates upper
  body and lower body

Caution
· Safe for most

Annotation Key
* indicates deep muscles

Grasp Sparrow's Tail: Push Left

Push helps you develop whole-body awareness. Perform this posture on a slightly slanting upward angle instead of pushing along a line parallel to the floor. The slight upward angle will allow you to push from the earth, through your legs and body, instead of just forcing it from your arms.

1 From Press, begin to shift your weight back onto your right leg. At the same time, imagine that your arms and hands become without substance for a moment. Your palms should face down, with the right above the left, and your arms separate, with your elbows floating down to your sides. Sink your elbows and shoulders, and face your palms downward, situated at the front of your hips. Your fingers should be lightly stretched.

2 Begin to rock your weight forward and allow your arms to push slightly forward so that your palms face out at the end of the movement. Keep a little slack in your arms and your elbows, and keep your shoulders down.

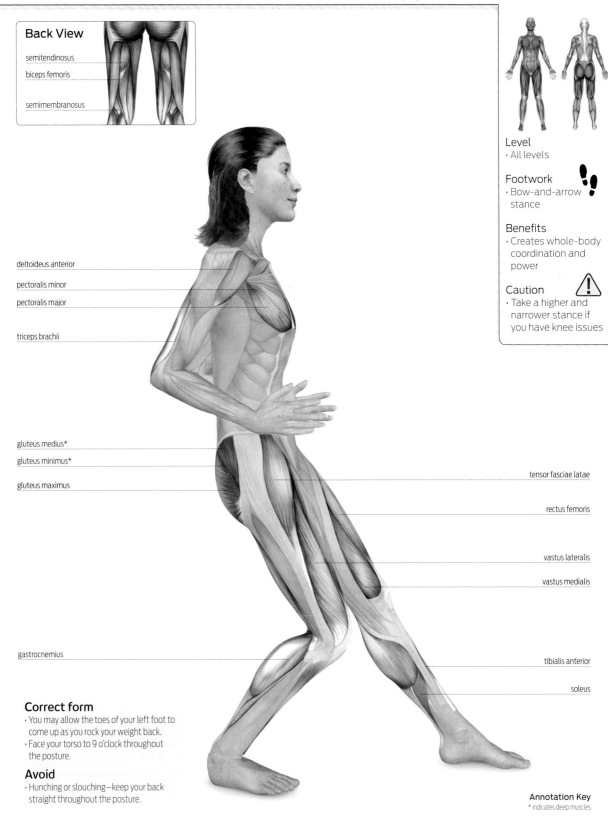

Back View

- semitendinosus
- biceps femoris
- semimembranosus

Level
· All levels

Footwork
· Bow-and-arrow stance

Benefits
· Creates whole-body coordination and power

Caution
· Take a higher and narrower stance if you have knee issues

deltoideus anterior

pectoralis minor

pectoralis major

triceps brachii

gluteus medius*

gluteus minimus*

gluteus maximus

gastrocnemius

tensor fasciae latae

rectus femoris

vastus lateralis

vastus medialis

tibialis anterior

soleus

Correct form
· You may allow the toes of your left foot to come up as you rock your weight back.
· Face your torso to 9 o'clock throughout the posture.

Avoid
· Hunching or slouching—keep your back straight throughout the posture.

Annotation Key
* indicates deep muscles

Grasp Sparrow's Tail: Transition

Use a hook step to transition into Grasp Sparrow's Tail for the right side. If you cannot hook in far enough, twine out your right foot a bit farther, then hook in your left a little more, and then sink back onto your left leg again.

1 From Push, shift your weight back onto your right leg, and let your arms "float" loosely at shoulder height. Hook your empty left foot inward and point your toes to approximately 2 o'clock. Rotate your arms so that your palms face out.

2 As you rotate your body to the right to face 12 o'clock, sweep your right hand out so that you arm is at face level, right elbow slightly bent.

3 Shift your weight down and then onto your left foot, torso facing 2 o'clock. Pull your right foot in next to the left as an empty step while you circle your right arm down to your left hip, palm up.

4 Put your left hand above, palm facing down, as if holding a large, lightweight sphere. Relax your shoulders and elbows downward.

Correct form
· To hook in farther, pick up your left foot, turn your toes inward by movement of your hip, and then set it down close to the right foot.
· Rotate your left leg as far inward as possible, in the hip, to make your left toes point in with the hook step. If you cannot do this yet, use a few twine and hook steps to turn your body approximately 180 degrees to protect your knee by keeping proper body alignment.

Avoid
· Pointing your left foot too far outward; instead, hook your foot farther inward to get into the correct position.

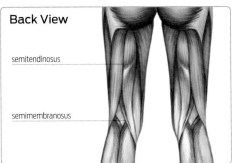

Back View

semitendinosus

semimembranosus

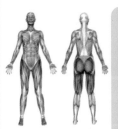

Level
· All levels

Footwork
· Empty stance
· Hook step

Benefits
· Releases lower back
· Energizes pelvic area

Caution
· Safe for most

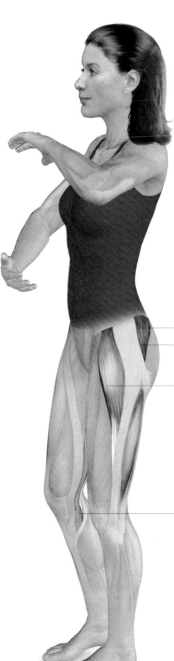

gluteus medius*

gluteus minimus*

tensor fasciae latae

gracilis*

Annotation Key
* indicates deep muscles

Grasp Sparrow's Tail: Ward Off Right

After completing Grasp Sparrow's Tail to the left, the transition puts you in the correct position to continue the sequence to the right, in mirror images of the previous postures. These photos and the ones you just viewed will help you to see all the angles of the movements. You again begin with Ward Off, which builds confidence and fortitude.

1 From Transition, your hands should be in line with the centerline of your torso, and your torso should be slightly rotated to the right.

2 Begin to step out your right heel, toes pointing to 3 o'clock. Slowly shift your weight onto your right foot to get into a bow-and-arrow stance. At the same time, let your arms "see-saw" apart, with your left hand pulling to your left hip, palm facing the floor, and right arm extending in front of you, arm held horizontally, palm facing you. As you do this, your torso rotates a little to the right, ending centered to 3 o'clock.

Correct form
· Sink your pelvis and imagine wrapping your right arm around a large, lightweight sphere.
· Keep your shoulders down and your head pulled straight.
· Slant your right elbow slightly downward.
· Firmly plant your feet.

Avoid
· Stepping out too far—keep your step the length of a normal large walking stride.
· Overextending or trying to reach out; instead, keep your arms within a comfortable range and "sit" into the posture.

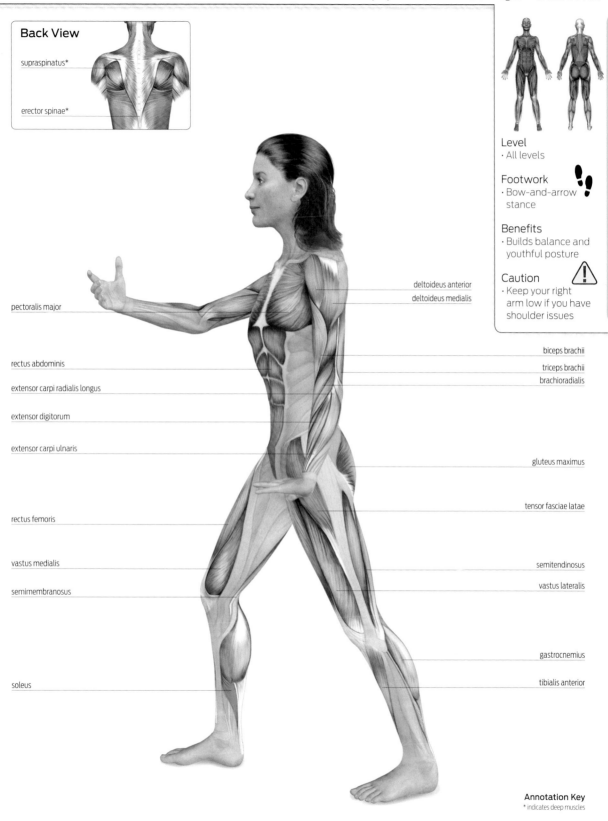

Back View

supraspinatus*

erector spinae*

deltoideus anterior
deltoideus medialis

pectoralis major

biceps brachii
triceps brachii
brachioradialis

rectus abdominis

extensor carpi radialis longus

extensor digitorum

extensor carpi ulnaris

gluteus maximus

tensor fasciae latae

rectus femoris

vastus medialis

semitendinosus
vastus lateralis

semimembranosus

gastrocnemius

soleus

tibialis anterior

Level
· All levels

Footwork
· Bow-and-arrow stance

Benefits
· Builds balance and youthful posture

Caution
· Keep your right arm low if you have shoulder issues

Annotation Key
* indicates deep muscles

Grasp Sparrow's Tail: Roll Back Right

Roll Back should always feel smooth. This posture teaches you how to properly position your lower back—overdoing it is just as bad as not doing enough. If you have stepped out too far in Ward Off, you will feel awkward when you shift back to start Roll Back. To correct your positioning, slide your left foot in as you shift back onto your right leg.

1 From Ward Off, turn your torso slightly to the left as you rotate your arm so that your palms face each other. Imagine that between your palms there is a very large, lightweight sphere or balloon.

2 Slowly shift your weight onto your left leg as your arms sweep down and then slightly upward. Your right hand will be at the height of your left armpit, and your left arm will be slightly extended out and back. Keep your elbows down, your pelvis tucked, and your left knee facing outward.

Correct form
· To avoid strain on your knees, keep your right knee facing out, tuck, and don't overdo it. Use straddle stretches to loosen your adductors.
· Tuck your pelvis as you finish this move to avoid pinching your lower back.

Avoid
· Sticking out your buttocks or leaning forward. Imagine that you are trying to sit straight onto your rear leg as you shift.
· Sweeping your arms too far back—this pulls too much on the spine.
· Overly rotating your body to the left.

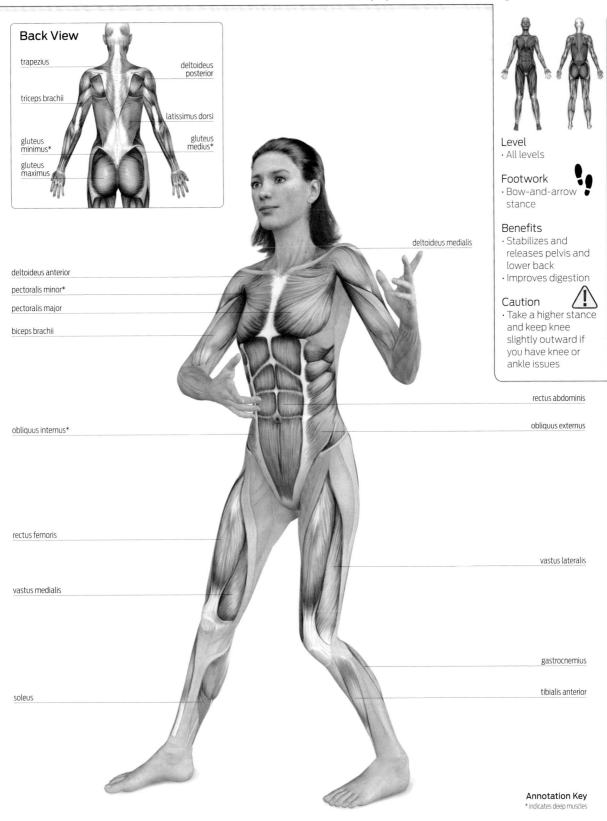

Back View

trapezius

deltoideus posterior

triceps brachii

latissimus dorsi

gluteus minimus*

gluteus medius*

gluteus maximus

deltoideus medialis

deltoideus anterior

pectoralis minor*

pectoralis major

biceps brachii

rectus abdominis

obliquus internus*

obliquus externus

rectus femoris

vastus lateralis

vastus medialis

gastrocnemius

tibialis anterior

soleus

Level
· All levels

Footwork
· Bow-and-arrow stance

Benefits
· Stabilizes and releases pelvis and lower back
· Improves digestion

Caution
· Take a higher stance and keep knee slightly outward if you have knee or ankle issues

Annotation Key
* indicates deep muscles

Grasp Sparrow's Tail: Press Right

In martial styles of tai chi chuan, Press is used in a close-in situation. It's therefore a rather compact posture. Just be sure that you don't confuse being compact with being crumpled up—watch your structure and hold it gracefully.

1 From Roll Back, start to shift forward, beginning to rotate your torso to again face 3 o'clock.

2 When your weight is equally distributed between both legs, bring the heels of your hand and wrist areas together to touch each other, forming a cross shape with your right hand on the outside and your left hand on the inside. The fingers of your right hand should be horizontal and the left fingers vertical, and your right arm will be more horizontal.

3 As you continue to shift forward onto your right leg, your torso continues to rotate to face 3 o'clock. At the end of the move, your hands should be in line with the centerline of your body, at chest level.

Correct form
· Imagine that there is a large, lightweight sphere between your arms.
· Sit comfortably into the posture.

Avoid
· Overextending; keep the rounded sphere shape between your arms and keep your shoulders and elbows relaxed downward.

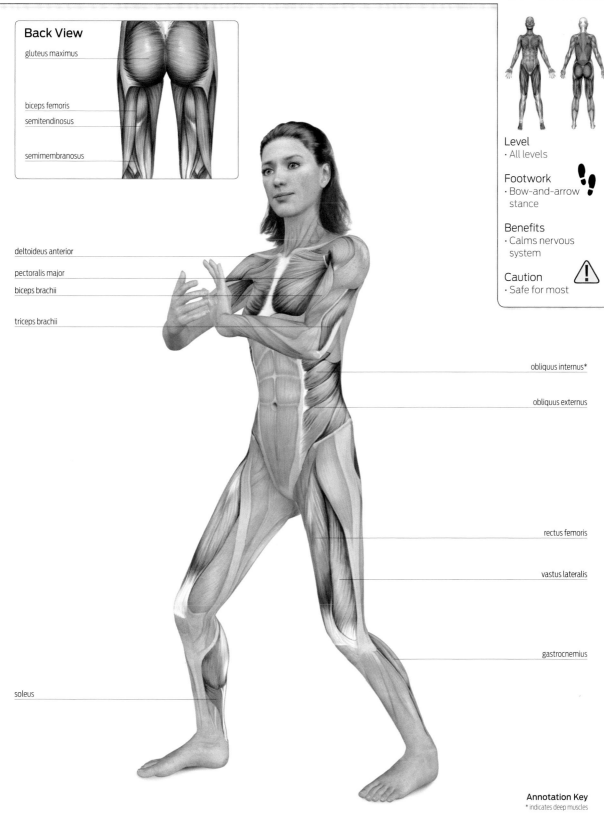

Back View

gluteus maximus

biceps femoris

semitendinosus

semimembranosus

deltoideus anterior

pectoralis major

biceps brachii

triceps brachii

obliquus internus*

obliquus externus

rectus femoris

vastus lateralis

gastrocnemius

soleus

Level
· All levels

Footwork
· Bow-and-arrow stance

Benefits
· Calms nervous system

Caution
· Safe for most

Annotation Key
* indicates deep muscles

Grasp Sparrow's Tail: Push Right

This is the same movement as the last Push (pages 38–39), only with your other foot forward. At the end of any Push, ensure that your elbows are relaxed downwardly. Doing both sides of the push—with the left foot forward as previously depicted, and here with the right foot forward—gives you an excellent exercise set to equalize your left and right sides.

1 From Press, begin to shift your weight back onto your left leg. At the same time, imagine that for a moment your arms and hands become without substance. Your palms should face down, with the left above the right, and your arms separate, with your elbows floating down gently to your sides. Sink your elbows and shoulders, and face your palms downward, situated at the front of your hips. Your fingers should be lightly stretched.

2 Begin to rock your weight forward and allow your arms to push slightly forward so that your palms face out at the end of the movement. Keep a little slack in your arms and your elbows, and keep your shoulders down.

Full-body anatomy

Front view
Annotation Key
* indicates deep muscles

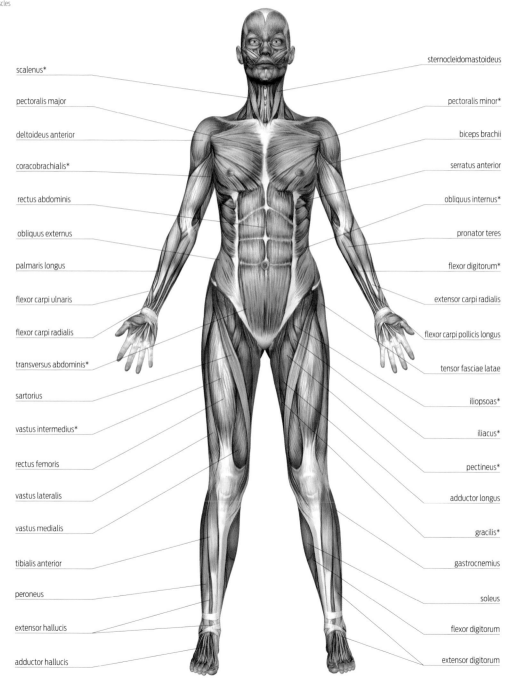

scalenus*

pectoralis major

deltoideus anterior

coracobrachialis*

rectus abdominis

obliquus externus

palmaris longus

flexor carpi ulnaris

flexor carpi radialis

transversus abdominis*

sartorius

vastus intermedius*

rectus femoris

vastus lateralis

vastus medialis

tibialis anterior

peroneus

extensor hallucis

adductor hallucis

sternocleidomastoideus

pectoralis minor*

biceps brachii

serratus anterior

obliquus internus*

pronator teres

flexor digitorum*

extensor carpi radialis

flexor carpi pollicis longus

tensor fasciae latae

iliopsoas*

iliacus*

pectineus*

adductor longus

gracilis*

gastrocnemius

soleus

flexor digitorum

extensor digitorum

Once you have familiarized yourself with the footwork, move on to postures. Section 1 takes you through the Yang 24 Short Form (pages 46–123), an excellent introduction to the essential elements of tai chi. By learning the Yang 24 Short Form, you will have enough tai chi knowledge to easily fit into various tai chi classes, workshops, and conventions. It also gives you a sense of confidence and completion.

Section 2 offers you a taste of the classic Chen Style with a series of movements excerpted from the form known as Xin Jia Pao Chui, or "New Frame Cannon Fist."

For the postures featured in both sections 1 and 2, you'll find a short introduction to the posture, step-by-step instructions explaining how to do it, some tips on correct form and what to avoid, and anatomical illustrations that show you just what muscles you are engaging. An at-a-glance sidebar gives you a fast visual references of the posture's target muscles, its level of difficulty, its benefits, and any cautions that may apply and what solution will work to overcome them. Also included is the key footwork—these are the steps and stances you need to know to tackle the posture. Work through the steps and stances, and then try the postures that require the steps you've mastered.

Don't rush through the postures; pick one or two to try at a time, and work on mastering them before you move on. As you learn individual postures, try putting them together. When you have mastered all the postures in a section, move through all of them in a smooth flowing sequence.

Learn to visualize

The step-by-step instructions will often ask you to visualize a certain image as you practice a posture, such as imagining that you are holding a large lightweight sphere or balloon between your hands. Learn to use these visualization cues to help you achieve the best possible positioning.

Finding time to practice

Tai chi masters have traditionally recommended an hour of practice per day. Along with tai chi form work, this hour may also include special exercises, breath work, and meditation. You can also work just on a small section of the form over and over again, until you know it well. The best answer is contained within you. Your inner self knows what it needs—it's up to you to start to listen to it.

The clock face

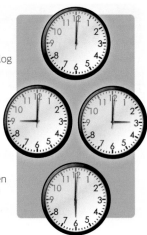

To help you understand directions and where to face, imagine your space as an analog clock face that stays fixed as you move. Your centerline points to the various numbers of the clock where the little hour hand would face. For example, you start your tai chi at 12:00. That means behind you is 6:00, to your right is 3:00, to your left is 9:00. If you face between 1:00 and 2:00, it's like the little hour hand being in between them at 1:30.

If you are short on time, exercise your creativity by seeking to employ tai chi principles in your day-to-day movements. Remember that tai chi is something you bring into your life. If you always keep it segregated from daily life, it will keep you segregated from all its benefits. Your goal is to make it an effortless practice and way of moving, thinking, feeling, and being. Always look for evidence and opportunities of it flowing into your body, mind, and life. Then you don't have to "do it"; instead, the tai chi "does you."

The tai chi tightrope

Tai chi requires one thing from you: the desire to develop your patience and diligence. If you are not willing to pay this price, you cannot reap the rewards. Tai chi is not a magic bullet. In the case of any pain or problem, of course, first check with your doctor, and then ask for clearance to engage in a practice of tai chi.

Next, be very logical about your practice. If you overdo it and hurt, next time, scale back on the intensity and watch the result. Increase the intensity as your energy rises and your body becomes increasingly conditioned. It is like commencing a practice of weight-lifting. Add more and more, little by little, and watch the result.

Underdoing your practice will lead to scanty or no results. Overdoing it will lead to pain or setbacks. Don't push yourself too hard, but don't be indolent either. And if you stop for a while, don't be discouraged or feel guilty. Forgive yourself and move on. Applaud yourself for the efforts and things you can do and did do, and refuse to berate yourself what you can't do or didn't do.

Keep a tai chi journal to record a minimum of five things you've seen improve over time, or five things you worked on to improve yourself with tai chi. Do not write a single negative thing. As the good thoughts collect, you will experience improvements in your quality of life.

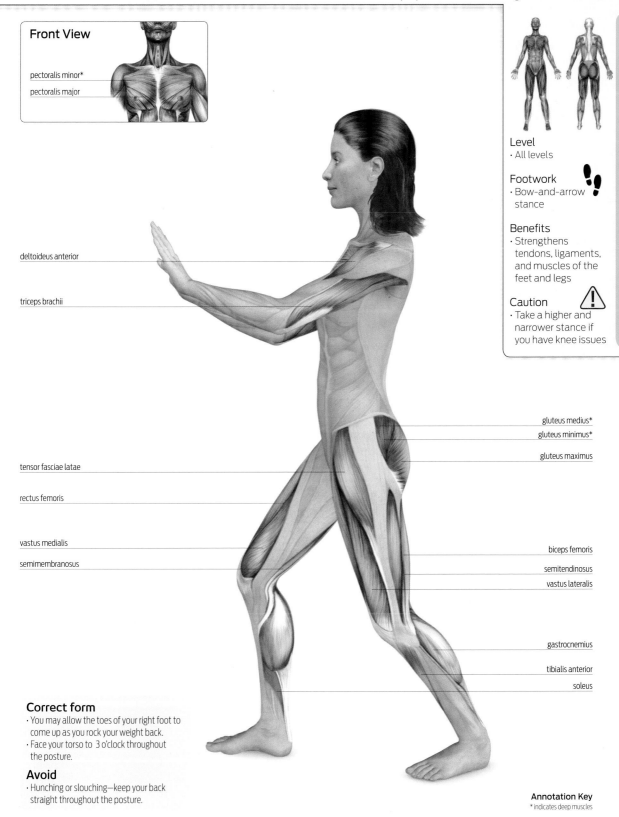

Front View

pectoralis minor*

pectoralis major

deltoideus anterior

triceps brachii

tensor fasciae latae

rectus femoris

vastus medialis

semimembranosus

gluteus medius*

gluteus minimus*

gluteus maximus

biceps femoris

semitendinosus

vastus lateralis

gastrocnemius

tibialis anterior

soleus

Level
· All levels

Footwork
· Bow-and-arrow stance

Benefits
· Strengthens tendons, ligaments, and muscles of the feet and legs

Caution
· Take a higher and narrower stance if you have knee issues

Correct form
· You may allow the toes of your right foot to come up as you rock your weight back.
· Face your torso to 3 o'clock throughout the posture.

Avoid
· Hunching or slouching—keep your back straight throughout the posture.

Annotation Key
* indicates deep muscles

Transition

This transition marks the beginning of Single Whip and turns your body leftward. Positioning the hook step in the right foot will determine where your end up.

1 From Push, shift your weight back onto your left leg. Lift the toes of your right foot, keeping your heel on the ground.

2 Hook your right foot inward by rotating in the right hip. Point your right toes to 12 o'clock.

3 While turning your body leftward, circle your arms to your left, as if you were turning the steering wheel of a car. Shift your weight to your right foot as your arms circle in closer, right arm higher and left lower.

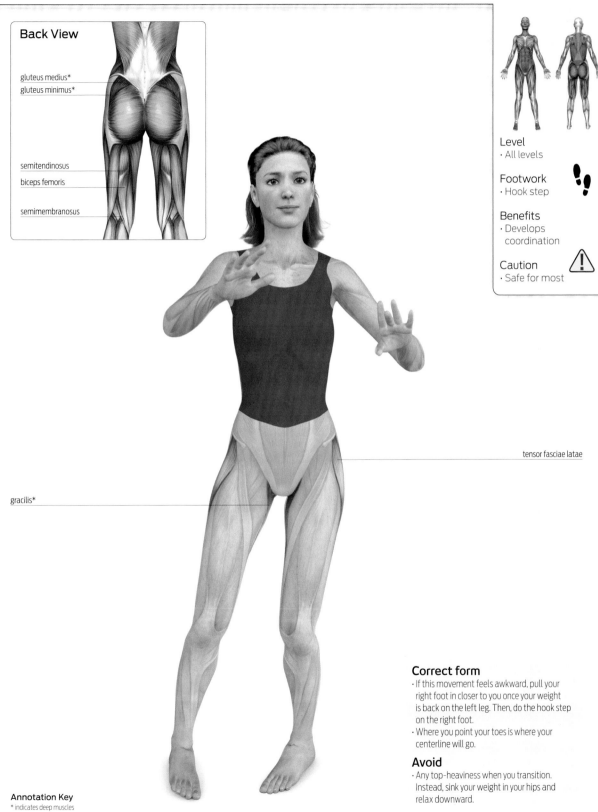

Back View

gluteus medius*
gluteus minimus*

semitendinosus
biceps femoris

semimembranosus

Level
· All levels

Footwork
· Hook step

Benefits
· Develops
  coordination

Caution
· Safe for most

tensor fasciae latae

gracilis*

Correct form

· If this movement feels awkward, pull your
  right foot in closer to you once your weight
  is back on the left leg. Then, do the hook step
  on the right foot.
· Where you point your toes is where your
  centerline will go.

Avoid

· Any top-heaviness when you transition.
  Instead, sink your weight in your hips and
  relax downward.

Annotation Key
* indicates deep muscles

Single Whip
(Part One)

Single Whip is present in every traditional tai chi chuan style. The rear hand forms a hook in which the wrist is bent and all the fingers touch, while the front hand is extended back, palm facing out. The bow-and-arrow stance forms the basis of this posture.

1 From Transition, as you move your arms, pull your left foot in as an empty step, next to your right foot.

2 As your right arm reaches shoulder height, extend it out to your right side, allowing your hand to become like a loose hook, with all fingers touching, pointing down, and your wrist bent.

3 Place your left hand palm up at the level of your right armpit level, with your elbow bent, facing down. The centerline of your torso faces between 1 and 2 o'clock. "Sit" onto your right leg.

Correct form
· Keep your arms stretched, yet slightly slack in the elbows.

Avoid
· Allowing your arms to crumple as you pull them closer to you. Always feel like your body is light and agile.
· Raising your shoulders.
· Protracting your head forward.
· Squatting too deeply if you have knee pain.

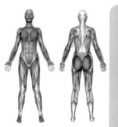

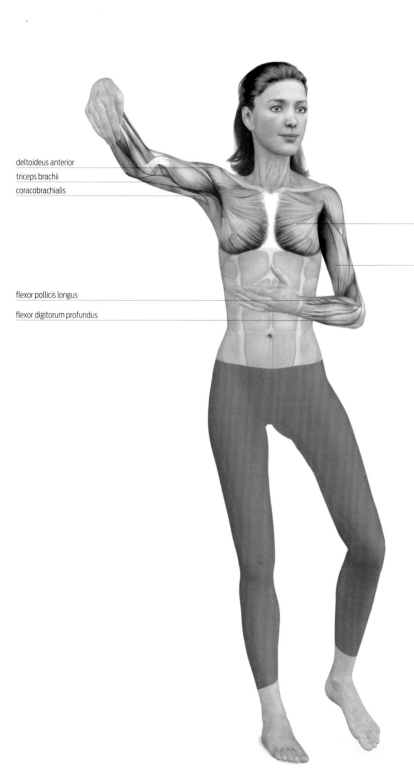

deltoideus anterior

triceps brachii

coracobrachialis

pectoralis major

biceps brachii

flexor pollicis longus

flexor digitorum profundus

Level
· All levels

Footwork
· Hook step
· Empty stance

Benefits
· Helps lymph circulation in upper body

Caution
· Ensure you're not crossing the back heel line if you have balance issues

Back View

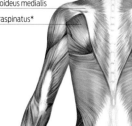

deltoideus medialis

supraspinatus*

Annotation Key
* indicates deep muscles

Single Whip
(Part Two)

From a compressed and narrow state, the Single Whip blossoms open into a fully expanded, large Yang Style tai chi posture. This posture appears twice in the Yang 24 Short Form—you'll repeat it again after the Cloud Hands series of postures (pages 90–93).

1 From Single Whip (Part One) begin to rotate your torso to 9 o'clock as you extend your left foot out and back, toes pointing to 9 o'clock, touching down on the heel first. Your left arm follows by extending out. Sink your weight.

2 Shift your weight onto your left foot. Continue to rotate your torso by using a hook step on the right heel when most of your weight is on the left foot.

3 At the same time, rotate your left arm so that your palm pushes out. Keep your shoulders pushed down, arms at equal height horizontally, with your elbows bent slightly to face down. About 60 to 70 percent of your weight is lunged forward onto your left leg as a bow-and-arrow step. Your arms should be even, approximately shoulder height, with your shoulders and elbows down.

Correct form
· Begin executing the twist step on the right foot only when most of your weight is on your left foot, and keep your left leg firmly fixed into position to offer a frame of support.
· At the end of the posture, extend for a moment, and then let your arms and legs go slightly slack.

Avoid
· Stepping the left leg out too widely.
· Overextending or slouching—sit comfortably into the posture.

Back View

deltoideus medialis

deltoideus posterior

supraspinatus*

teres major

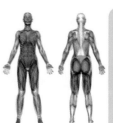

Level
· All levels

Footwork
· L-stance
· Twist step,
· Bow-and-arrow stance

Benefits
· Enhances whole-body *qi* and lymphatic circulation

Caution
· Ensure you're not crossing the back heel line if you have balance issues

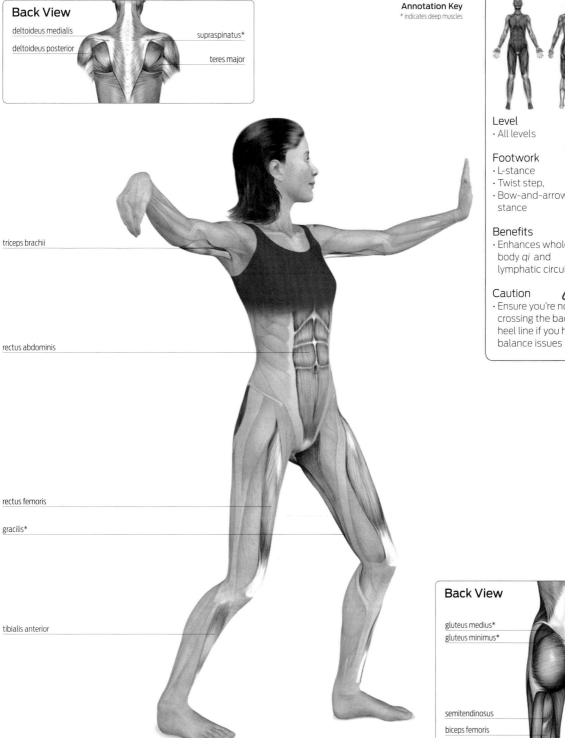

triceps brachii

rectus abdominis

rectus femoris

gracilis*

tibialis anterior

Back View

gluteus medius*

gluteus minimus*

semitendinosus

biceps femoris

semimembranosus

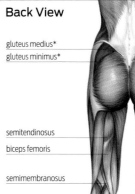

Cloud Hands
(Part One)

Cloud Hands symbolizes the cyclical rising and setting of the sun and moon. Note how the arms are held in a spherical shape. The rhythm of this movement, the stepping down of the foot, signals the turn of the sphere. From yin to yang and yang to yin, stepping slowly like the passing of time.

1 Shift your weight onto your right leg. Pivot on your left heel to hook step, so that your toes point to 12 o'clock.

2 By turning in the *kua*, rotate your torso to the right as your left arm sweeps to the right. Unhook your right hand. Notice that the weight is on your right leg and your arms are to the right.

3 Face your torso to 12 o'clock as you shift your weight to the left, while sweeping your left arm across your body to the left and your right arm down in front of you, palm up at waist level. When your hands reach the centerline of your body, equalize your weight on both feet in a horse stance. Imagine that you are holding a large balloon or lightweight sphere.

4 With your pelvis gently tucked and your elbows relaxed downward, shift slightly more to the left, pointing your right toes forward, pivoting on the heel.

Correct form
· Make sure you are truly shifting your weight to move the "sphere," instead of just moving your arms independently.
· Keep your feet parallel throughout this move.

Avoid
· Overextending your arms out to the side as you shift your weight.

5 Shift all your weight to the left, twisting your torso leftward. Extend your arms to the left, and bring your right foot in, parallel and next to your left foot.

6 As you commence placing weight onto your right foot, switch your arm position as if turning over the sphere: your left arm sweeps down at waist level, palm up, and your right arm sweeps up at shoulder height, palm down.

7 Start to shift your weight slightly to the right so that you are in a balanced horse stance facing 12 o'clock. Move the imaginary sphere to hold it at the centerline of your torso.

8 Continue shifting weight onto your right foot while turning your torso slightly to the right. Let your arms extend out slightly to the right, so that all your body weight is on your right foot. This completes Part One.

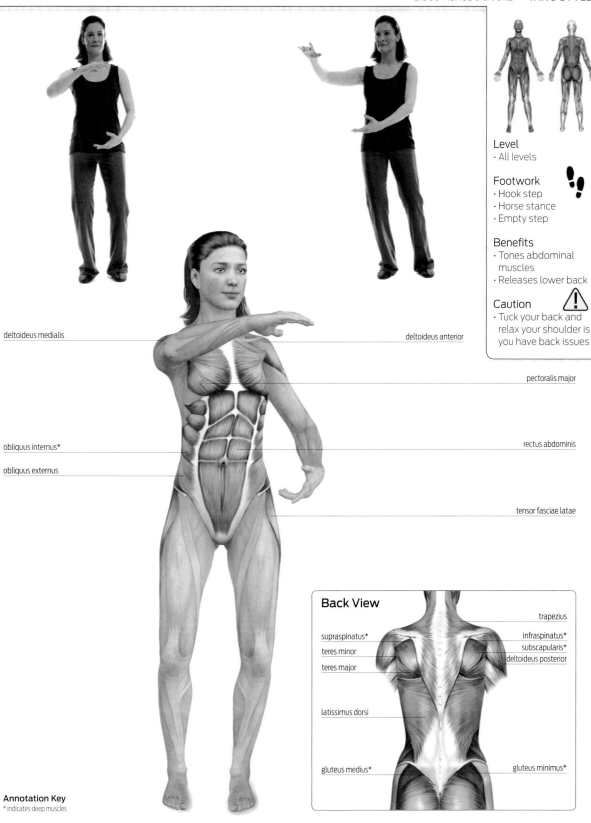

Level
· All levels

Footwork
· Hook step
· Horse stance
· Empty step

Benefits
· Tones abdominal muscles
· Releases lower back

Caution
· Tuck your back and relax your shoulder is you have back issues

deltoideus medialis

deltoideus anterior

pectoralis major

obliquus internus*

rectus abdominis

obliquus externus

tensor fasciae latae

Back View

trapezius

supraspinatus*

infraspinatus*

teres minor

subscapularis*

teres major

deltoideus posterior

latissimus dorsi

gluteus medius*

gluteus minimus*

Annotation Key
* indicates deep muscles

Cloud Hands
(Part Two and Part Three)

As you emulate the rising and setting of the sun and moon, think about this: Is the sun really moving up and down over the horizon? The turning of the earth causes this illusion. This posture reminds us to think more deeply about our understanding of the truth. Express the natural truth of this posture by using your whole body as one unit—that is the true source of the movement of the arms turning the sphere, not the independent movement of the arms.

1 Step your left foot to the left to widen your horse stance. As you set your foot down, turn over the sphere again; your right hand shifts to the bottom and your left hand comes to the top, palms facing each other.

2 Start shifting your weight to the left. When your weight is distributed equally on both legs, hold the sphere at the centerline of your body. Continue shifting leftward and extending your arms to the left when all your weight is on the left.

3 As you commence placing weight onto your right foot, switch your arm position as if turning over the sphere: your left arm sweeps down at waist level, palm up, and your right arm sweeps up at shoulder height, palm down.

4 Start to shift your weight slightly to the right so that you are in a balanced horse stance facing 12 o'clock. Move the imaginary sphere to hold it at the centerline of your torso.

5 Continue shifting weight onto your right foot while turning your torso slightly to the right. Let your arms extend out slightly to the right, so that all your body weight is on your right foot. This completes Part Two.

6 Repeat all steps to complete Part Three, and as you finish, allow your right hand to fall into a hook. Continue on to perform another Single Whip (pages 86–89).

Correct form
· Make sure you are truly shifting your weight to move the "sphere," instead of just moving your arms independently.
· Keep your feet parallel throughout this move.

Avoid
· Insufficiently tucking your pelvis, which may result in lower-back or knee soreness.

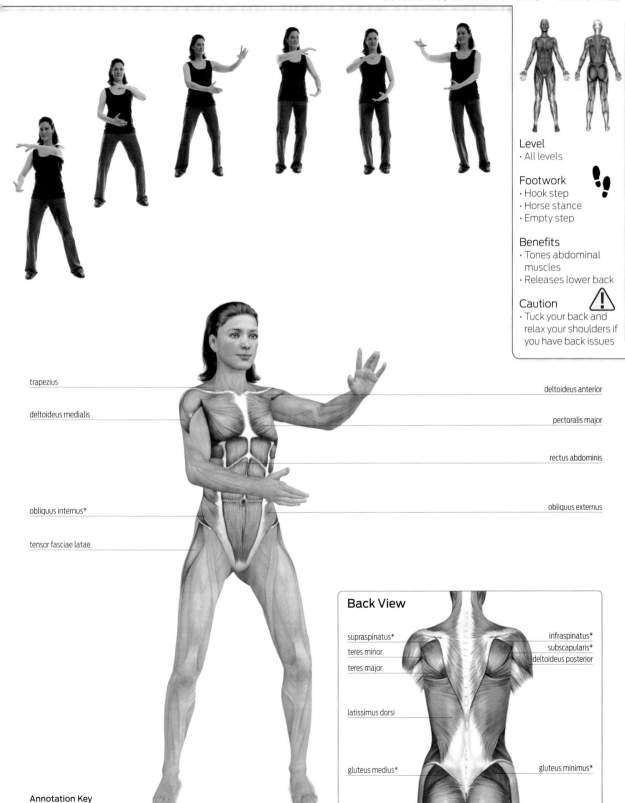

Level
· All levels

Footwork
· Hook step
· Horse stance
· Empty step

Benefits
· Tones abdominal muscles
· Releases lower back

Caution
· Tuck your back and relax your shoulders if you have back issues

trapezius

deltoideus medialis

obliquus internus*

tensor fasciae latae

deltoideus anterior

pectoralis major

rectus abdominis

obliquus externus

Back View

supraspinatus*

teres minor

teres major

latissimus dorsi

gluteus medius*

infraspinatus*

subscapularis*

deltoideus posterior

gluteus minimus*

Annotation Key
* indicates deep muscles

High Pat on Horse

Many people mistakenly teach that the High Pat on Horse tai chi posture mimics the right hand reaching up to pat a horse's neck. The truth is that this posture is mistranslated from its Chinese name *Gao Tan Ma*, which refers to a high-ranking mounted scout. Like a high-ranking scout mounted on a horse, sit into the posture relaxed but alert.

1 From Single Whip, release your right hooked hand and rotate your arms to face your palms upward. Shift your weight to your left leg. Bring your right foot forward with a half step as you slightly turn your torso rightward and bring your right hand near your right ear, palm facing forward and elbow down.

2 Shift your weight back onto your right leg by pushing off from your left foot. As you push off, turn your torso leftward to face 9 o'clock. At the same time, push your left hand down to your left hip with palm up, and slowly push your right palm forward.

3 Keep your elbows relaxed down as your left foot finishes as an empty step.

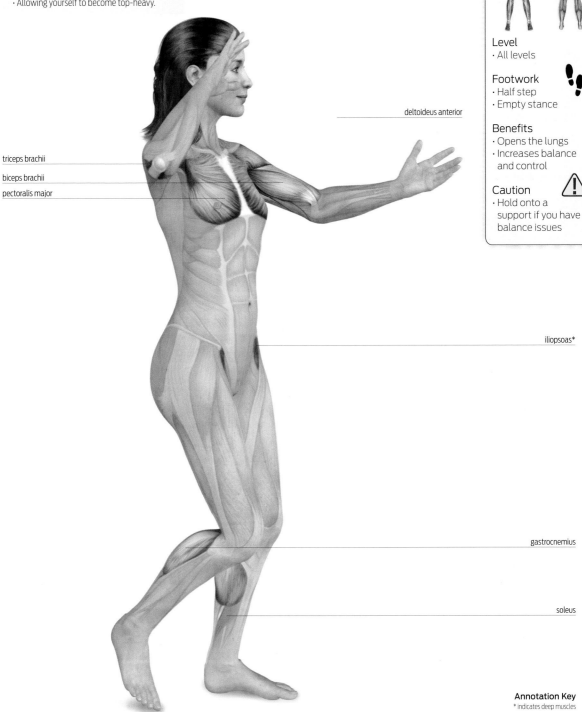

Correct form
· Keep your center of gravity down by relaxing your chest and imagining you are sitting on a high stool.

Avoid
· Allowing yourself to become top-heavy.

deltoideus anterior

triceps brachii

biceps brachii

pectoralis major

Level
· All levels

Footwork
· Half step
· Empty stance

Benefits
· Opens the lungs
· Increases balance and control

Caution
· Hold onto a support if you have balance issues

iliopsoas*

gastrocnemius

soleus

Annotation Key
* indicates deep muscles

Kick Right Foot

Tai chi postures are traditionally named for the move they finish into instead of the movement that begins the posture. Kick Right Foot is a good example—several movements lead to the culmination of the posture in the kick. Each movement is vitally important to the end result. Like tai chi chuan, everything in life is much the same—all actions you take now will influence the future result. Use mindfulness in all actions.

1 Cross the back of your right wrist under the back of your left hand. Your hands should be at shoulder height in front of your centerline and your elbows should be down. Begin to separate your hands outward and downward as you step your left foot out to about 8 o'clock.

2 As you lower your weight onto your left leg, sweep both hands inward and upward so that the hands cross with your right on the outside. Pull your right foot in at the same time. Lift your right knee into a rooster stance.

3 Keeping your back straight, kick to 10 o'clock as you spread your arms upward and out to the sides. Keep your right arm aligned with your right leg, and point your toes up when kicking with the heel. Imagine that you are sitting on your left leg when kicking your right.

4 At the end of the kick, retract your right leg into a rooster stance, and retract your arms to shoulder height. Your elbows should be slightly bent and facing down, with your palms facing your body.

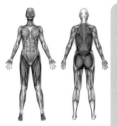

Back View

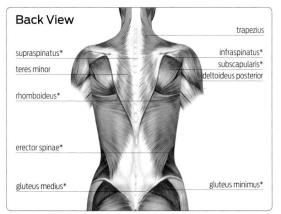

- trapezius
- supraspinatus*
- infraspinatus*
- teres minor
- subscapularis*
- deltoideus posterior
- rhomboideus*
- erector spinae*
- gluteus medius*
- gluteus minimus*

Level
- All levels

Footwork
- Empty stance
- Rooster stance

Benefits
- Increases balance, flexibility, strength, and endurance

Caution
- Hold onto a support and just lift your foot for a moment if you have balance issues

Annotation Key
* indicates deep muscles

- teres major
- latissimus dorsi
- piriformis*
- gluteus maximus
- obturator externus*
- rectus femoris

Correct form
- Keep your arms positioned so that your right arm is in line with your right leg during the kick.
- Always pull kicks back into a rooster stance.
- If you can't hold your leg up in the kick, just touch your toe down as lightly on the floor as possible, and hold for 5 to 10 seconds. This will help improve your balance.

Avoid
- Lifting your leg higher than is comfortable.

Front View

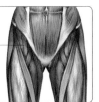

- iliopsoas*

Double Strike Opponent's Ears

Double Strike Opponent's Ears is a wonderful study in seeking the harmony of yin and yang. It calls for you to lunge forward, but you must remember not to overextend. You must reach overhead, but you must be careful not to reach too high. You reach your arms out, but you must keep your elbows relaxed. After the perceived "strike," you must loosen your fists.

1 Lower your elbows down to your thighs. With palms up, form loose fists. Step your right heel out to about 10 o'clock, with all your weight still on your left leg.

2 Begin to arc your arms outward, upward, and overhead as you lunge onto your right leg. As you finish this move, turn your fists downward as your reach your hands overhead to about eye level to execute a double strike. You are now facing to approximately 10 o'clock.

Correct form
· Keep your thumbs curled over your fingers when making fists.
· Make sure that the strike and the lunge occur simultaneously.

Avoid
· Overextending your knee and arms.
· Lunging too far forward; keep your right knee behind the vertical line of your right toes.

Back View

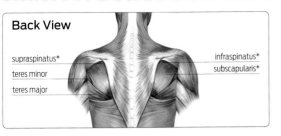

supraspinatus*

teres minor

teres major

infraspinatus*

subscapularis*

Level
· All levels

Footwork
· Empty stance
· Bow-and-arrow stance

Benefits
· Energizes the body
· Tones the arms

Caution ⚠
· Do not lunge too far forward if you have knee pain
· Keep your arms low if you have shoulder issues

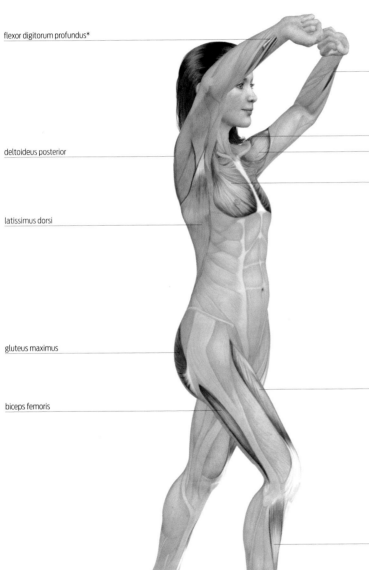

flexor digitorum profundus*

flexor digitorum superficialis

deltoideus medialis

deltoideus anterior

pectoralis major

deltoideus posterior

latissimus dorsi

gluteus maximus

rectus femoris

biceps femoris

tibialis anterior

Annotation Key
* indicates deep muscles

Turn Body and Kick Left Foot

Turn Body and Kick Left Foot reminds you how well the Yang 24 Short Form tai chi chuan develops both the left and right sides of your body. It was thoughtfully planned to give you the perfect balance of left- and right-side movements. In the next set of postures, you will also see how the Yang 24 Short Form also gives you a thorough workout, moving between very high and very low postures.

1 Shift your weight back onto your left leg as you open your fists and slightly lower your elbows. Lift your right toes so that you can pivot on your heel, inwardly rotating your right leg so that your toes point to 7 o'clock.

2 Extend your arms out to shoulder height, and then continue to circle them down to front of your body, crossing your left hand over your right, at your center. Shift all your weight onto your right leg, and draw in your left foot as an empty step.

3 Raise your hands to about shoulder height as you bring your left knee up into a rooster stance. Kick to 4:30 as you spread your arms upward and out to the sides, palms facing out.

4 Keep your left toes pointed up when kicking with the heel. Feel like you are sitting on your right leg when kicking the left.

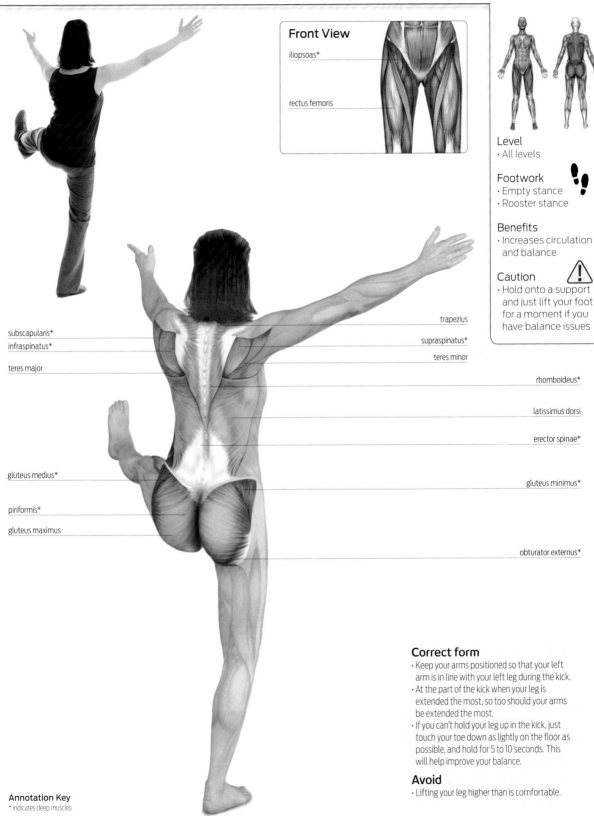

Front View

iliopsoas*

rectus femoris

Level
· All levels

Footwork
· Empty stance
· Rooster stance

Benefits
· Increases circulation and balance

Caution
· Hold onto a support and just lift your foot for a moment if you have balance issues

trapezius

subscapularis*

infraspinatus*

supraspinatus*

teres major

teres minor

rhomboideus*

latissimus dorsi

erector spinae*

gluteus medius*

gluteus minimus*

piriformis*

gluteus maximus

obturator externus*

Correct form
· Keep your arms positioned so that your left arm is in line with your left leg during the kick.
· At the part of the kick when your leg is extended the most, so too should your arms be extended the most.
· If you can't hold your leg up in the kick, just touch your toe down as lightly on the floor as possible, and hold for 5 to 10 seconds. This will help improve your balance.

Avoid
· Lifting your leg higher than is comfortable.

Annotation Key
* indicates deep muscles

Snake Creeps Down and Golden Pheasant Stands on One Leg Left

In tai chi chuan combat training, the Snake Creeps Down and Golden Pheasant Stands on One Leg set of postures would first be executed very slowly, several times a day, for at least a month. This builds up the tendons, ligaments, and stabilizer muscles. Gradually, the movements would be sped up as fast as possible—the practitioner would develop incredible plyometric strength and strong white fiber, fast-twitch muscles. Once you are conditioned and pain free, you can give this old methodology a try.

1 Retract the left kick into a rooster stance. Form a hook with your right hand and extend your right arm as in Single Whip (pages 86–89) with your elbow gently bent and facing down. Turn your torso slightly to the right as you sweep your left hand down across your body and up in front of your right shoulder. You are now facing 7 o'clock.

2 Squat on your right leg as you twist your torso leftward, and stretch your left leg out to 3 o'clock, with your toes pointing to 6 o'clock in a tiger stance.

3 Extend your left arm, and slide the back of your left hand down along the inner side of your straight left leg. At the same time, twist out your left foot, pivoting on the heel to point the toes to 3 o'clock, while slowly shifting your weight to your left foot.

4 Raise your left arm to shoulder height while you shift your weight forward onto your left leg. Lower your right arm and put it behind you, with a hooked hand, fingers facing up.

5 Twist step to turn your right toes inward as you end up in a bow-and-arrow stance facing 3 o'clock.

6 Push your left arm down to your hip, palm down as you bring in your right foot and then raise your knee in a rooster stance. Raise your right hand up in front of you, palm facing to the left, fingers up.

Correct form
· Lift yourself from the *kua* when coming up from the tiger stance to protect your knees, adductors, and hamstrings.
· To perform this posture in a higher stance, slide out your left arm well above your left leg as you twist your torso and shift your weight.
· When you rise up into the rooster stance, tuck your pelvis and keep your head and back as straight as possible.

Avoid
· Crouching lower in tiger stance than you can while still maintaining close to upright posture.

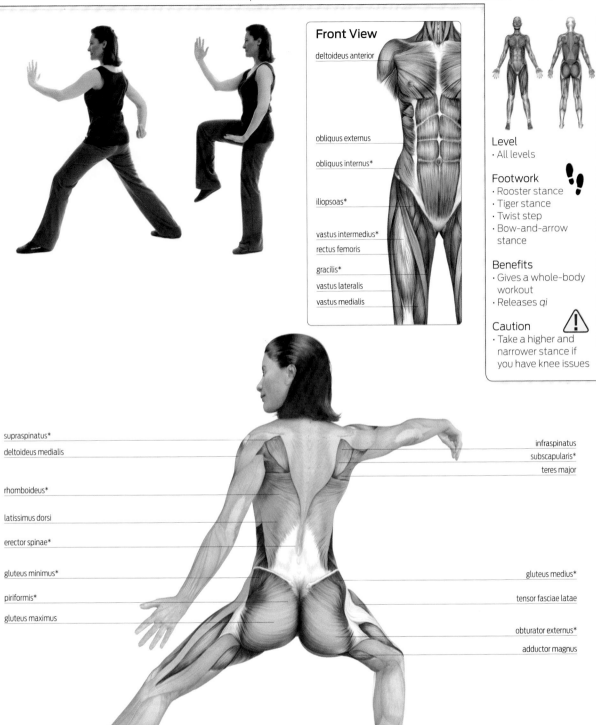

Front View

deltoideus anterior

obliquus externus

obliquus internus*

iliopsoas*

vastus intermedius*

rectus femoris

gracilis*

vastus lateralis

vastus medialis

Level
· All levels

Footwork
· Rooster stance
· Tiger stance
· Twist step
· Bow-and-arrow stance

Benefits
· Gives a whole-body workout
· Releases *qi*

Caution
· Take a higher and narrower stance if you have knee issues

supraspinatus*

deltoideus medialis

rhomboideus*

latissimus dorsi

erector spinae*

gluteus minimus*

piriformis*

gluteus maximus

infraspinatus

subscapularis*

teres major

gluteus medius*

tensor fasciae latae

obturator externus*

adductor magnus

Annotation Key
* indicates deep muscles

Snake Creeps Down and Golden Pheasant Stands on One Leg Right

The Yang 24 Short Form tai chi chuan sometimes labels this posture as "Lower the Body and Stand on One Leg." This set of movements is an intense contrast of low and high postures. You can make it much higher if you have joint pain, or you can go very low and high if you are in the condition to do so.

1 Set your right foot down as an empty hook step with your toes pointing to 12 o'clock. Shift all your weight onto your right foot. As you finish shifting, pivot on the heel of your empty left foot to point your toes to 12 o'clock. Then shift all your weight back onto your left foot.

2 Extend your left arm up and to the left with your hand as a hook. Sweep your right arm across your body and in front of your left shoulder. Draw in your right foot as an empty step.

3 Squat on your left leg as you twist your torso rightward, and stretch your right leg out to 3 o'clock, with toes pointing to 12 o'clock in a tiger stance.

4 Extend your right arm and slide the back of your right hand down along the inner side of your straight right leg. At the same time, twist out your right foot, pivoting on the heel, to point your toes to 3 o'clock, while slowly shifting your weight to your right foot.

5 Raise your right arm to shoulder height while you shift your weight forward onto your right leg. Lower your left arm and put it behind you, with a hooked hand, fingers facing up.

6 Twist step to turn your left toes inward as you end up in a bow-and-arrow stance facing 3 o'clock.

7 Push your right arm down to your hip, palm down, as you bring in your left foot and then raise your knee in a rooster stance. Raise your left hand up in front of you, palm facing to the right, fingers up.

Correct form
- Lift yourself from the *kua* when coming up from the tiger stance to protect your knees, adductors, and hamstrings.
- To perform this posture in a higher stance, slide out your left arm well above your left leg as you twist your torso and shift your weight.
- When you rise up into the rooster stance, tuck your pelvis and keep your head and back as straight as possible.

Avoid
- Crouching lower in tiger stance than you can while still maintaining close to upright posture.

Back View

supraspinatus*
teres minor
teres major

infraspinatus*
subscapularis*
deltoideus posterior

rhomboideus*

latissimus dorsi

erector spinae*

gluteus medius*

gluteus minimus*

piriformis*

gluteus maximus

obturator externus*

Level
· All levels

Footwork
· Rooster stance
· Tiger stance
· Twist step
· Bow-and-arrow stance

Benefits
· Gives a whole-body workout

Caution
· Take a higher and narrower stance if you have knee issues

deltoideus anterior

deltoideus medialis

obliquus externus
obliquus internus*
rectus femoris

tensor fasciae latae
iliopsoas*
vastus intermedius*
vastus lateralis

gracilis*
adductor magnus

vastus medialis

Annotation Key
* indicates deep muscles

Fair Lady Threads Shuttles Right

Fair Lady Threads Shuttles is named after women working on their weaving looms. The shuttle carried the weft thread and would be thrown across the warp threads of the loom. Then the warp was switched and the weft would be shuttled across in the other direction. In the traditional Yang Long Form, this posture is repeated four times to the four corners. Here, it is repeated twice to adjacent corners.

1 Turn your torso to the left as you step your left foot down to 2 o'clock. While stepping down, draw your hands in front of your torso as if you are holding a sphere with your right hand below and left hand above, palms facing each other.

2 Draw in your right foot emptily. Turn your torso to the right as you extend your right leg to step out, heel first, to 4 o'clock.

3 As you step out, raise your right forearm. Keeping your arm rounded, begin to shift forward onto your right leg while using a twist step of your left foot to put you in a bow-and-arrow stance.

4 Extend your left palm forward with elbow down. At same time, rotate your right palm to face out. End with your right palm at forehead height and your left palm out at eye level. You are now facing 4 o'clock

Front View

deltoideus anterior

pectoralis minor*

pectoralis major

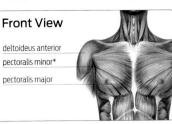

Level
· All levels

Footwork
· Empty stance
· L-stance
· Twist step
· Bow-and-arrow
 stance

Benefits
· Normalizes
 circulation
· Strengthens upper
 and lower body

Caution
· Safe for most

infraspinatus*

teres minor

extensor digitorum communis

triceps brachii

serratus anterior

piriformis*

gluteus maximus

tensor fasciae latae

rectus femoris

biceps femoris

vastus lateralis

Correct form
· Use L-stances and twist steps to get you
 to face the corners when you execute this
 movement.

Avoid
· Twisting from the knee, rather than the *kua*.
· Overextending your front knee.

Annotation Key
* indicates deep muscles

Fair Lady Threads Shuttles Left

Fair Lady Threads Shuttles emphasizes a recurring pattern in the Yang 24 Short Form: whenever you hold an imaginary spherical structure in your hands and arms, the bottom arm is the one that comes up and out in the following movement. As you do more tai chi chuan, you will recognize additional patterns—not just in tai chi or physical movement, but in everyday life as well.

1 Shift all your weight onto your right leg, and draw in your left foot as an empty step. Turn your torso slightly to the right and face your palms to each other as you bring your hands in front of your abdomen as if holding a sphere with your right hand on top and left at the bottom.

2 Start turning your torso to the left as you extend your left leg to step out, heel first, to 2 o'clock. As you extend your leg, begin to raise your left forearm, keeping your arm rounded.

3 Shift forward onto your left leg, using a twist step of your right foot to puts you in a bow-and-arrow stance.

4 Extend your right palm forward with elbow down while rotating your left palm to face out. End with your left palm at forehead height and right palm out at eye level. You are now facing 2 o'clock.

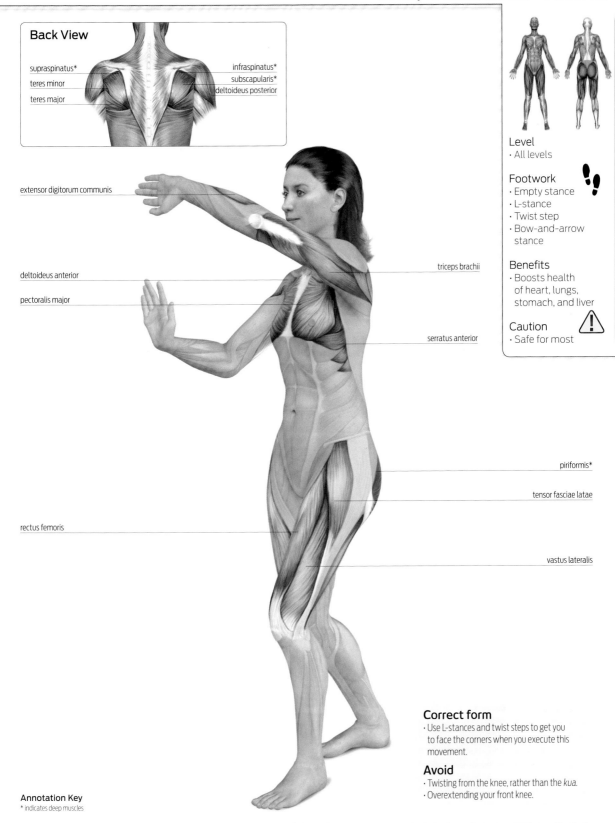

Back View

supraspinatus*
teres minor
teres major

infraspinatus*
subscapularis*
deltoideus posterior

extensor digitorum communis

deltoideus anterior

pectoralis major

triceps brachii

serratus anterior

rectus femoris

piriformis*

tensor fasciae latae

vastus lateralis

Level
· All levels

Footwork
· Empty stance
· L-stance
· Twist step
· Bow-and-arrow
  stance

Benefits
· Boosts health
  of heart, lungs,
  stomach, and liver

Caution
· Safe for most

Correct form
· Use L-stances and twist steps to get you
  to face the corners when you execute this
  movement.

Avoid
· Twisting from the knee, rather than the *kua*.
· Overextending your front knee.

Annotation Key
* indicates deep muscles

Needle at Sea Bottom

Controversy surrounds the origin of the name of this posture. Needle at Sea Bottom possibly comes from an old Chinese story in which a magical staff could be made small as a needle to easily conceal it. Other stories mention how the lower part of an opponent's body was referred to as "sea bottom," and the martial application referred to the hand "stabbing" to this area. Other stories suggest an intent that must be strong enough to pick up a needle even from the depths of the sea. Whatever its meaning, this posture develops the body and energetic use of good structure.

1 Using a half step, bring the inside edge of your right foot just behind your left heel. Face 3 o'clock, and shift your weight back onto your right foot.

2 Lower your arms in front of you, extending your right arm down in front at a 45-degree angle, thumb up.

3 Brush your left palm down your right forearm as you lift your left foot slightly off the floor. Continue pushing your left hand downward as you circle your right palm back, behind, and up until it is near your right ear. Extend out your left foot to 3 o'clock, toes on the floor as an empty step.

4 Keeping all your weight on your right leg, thrust your right fingers down on a 45-degree angle, thumb up, and pull your left hand to your hip, palm down. You are now squatting on your right leg.

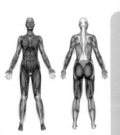

Correct form
· Keep your right knee aligned with your right
 toes so that the knee is not torqued.

Avoid
· Leaning forward as you lower into the squat.

Level
· All levels

Footwork
· Half step
· Empty stance

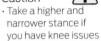

Benefits
· Improves spinal
 alignment
· Boosts health of
 abdominal organs

Caution
· Take a higher and
 narrower stance if
 you have knee issues
· Hold onto a
 support if you have
 balance issues

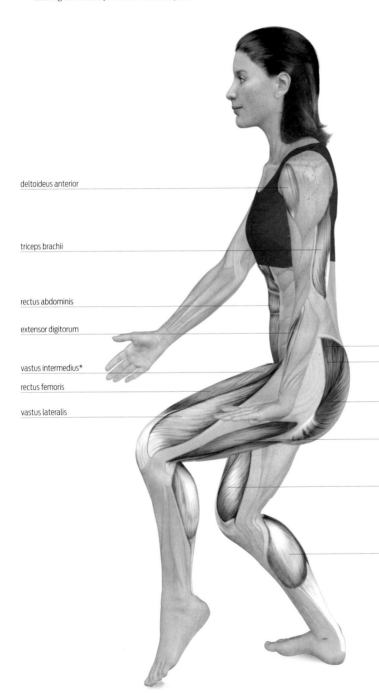

deltoideus anterior

triceps brachii

rectus abdominis

extensor digitorum

vastus intermedius*

rectus femoris

vastus lateralis

gluteus medius*

gluteus minimus*

gluteus maximus

biceps femoris

vastus medialis

gastrocnemius

Annotation Key
* indicates deep muscles

Fan through the Back

Like a fan hinged and unfolding, notice how the movement blossoms open from a narrow beginning to an expanded finish. To prevent top-heaviness, be sure to pay careful attention to rooting in your stance. At the end of the movement, your structure must be impeccable—ears in line with shoulders, lower back tucked, chest energy relaxed inward and downward, and fingers lightly stretched.

1 Turn your torso slightly to the right as you rotate your palms upward, raising your arms to about chin height. Begin to turn your palms to face each other, keeping your elbows down.

2 Raise your left leg into a rooster stance, and then step your left foot forward to 3 o'clock, touching your heel first. As you shift forward into a bow-and-arrow stance, twist your right palm outward as you pull it next to your right ear, and push your left palm out, extending your left arm in front of you.

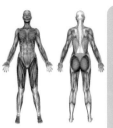

Front View

iliopsoas*

Level
· All levels

Footwork
· Rooster stance
· Empty stance
· Bow-and-arrow stance

Benefits
· Increases confidence
· Improves balance
· Stabilizes back

Caution
· Keep your arms lower if you have shoulder issues

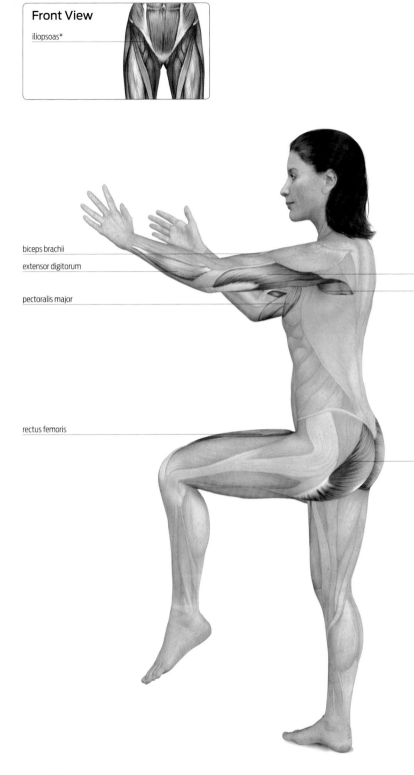

biceps brachii

extensor digitorum

pectoralis major

rectus femoris

triceps brachii

teres major

gluteus maximus

Correct form
· When you rise up into the rooster stance, tuck your pelvis and keep your head and back as straight as possible.

Avoid
· Stooping over to do this posture—if you have knee pain, keep a higher stance.

Annotation Key
* indicates deep muscles

Turn Body and Deflect

The hook step again comes into play in Turn Body and Deflect. Make sure that after you turn your body, your left toes are pointing almost 180 degrees from where they were at the end of Fan through the Back. If you cannot rotate that much in your *kua*, use a series of twine and hook steps to get you there. There is no excuse for commencing a tai chi posture from a poor stance—fix your stances in order to carry the flow of the movement properly and to avoid injury.

1 To perform Turn Body, shift your weight back onto your right leg and let your arms sweep overhead in a slight clockwise arc as you twist in your left *kua* to hook step your left toes inward. Then shift all your weight onto your left leg.

2 Finish turning your torso to the right as you make a fist with your right hand, palm down, as you draw it downward in front of your left lower ribs. Pull your right in as an empty step.

3 To continue on to Deflect, arc your left forearm down in front of your body, outside of your right fist (palm down), to your abdomen. Then pull it to your left hip while you extend your right leg forward emptily on the heel. Your right fist arcs up clockwise and slightly to the right. As you move your fist to the right, simultaneously rotate your right leg outward from the *kua*.

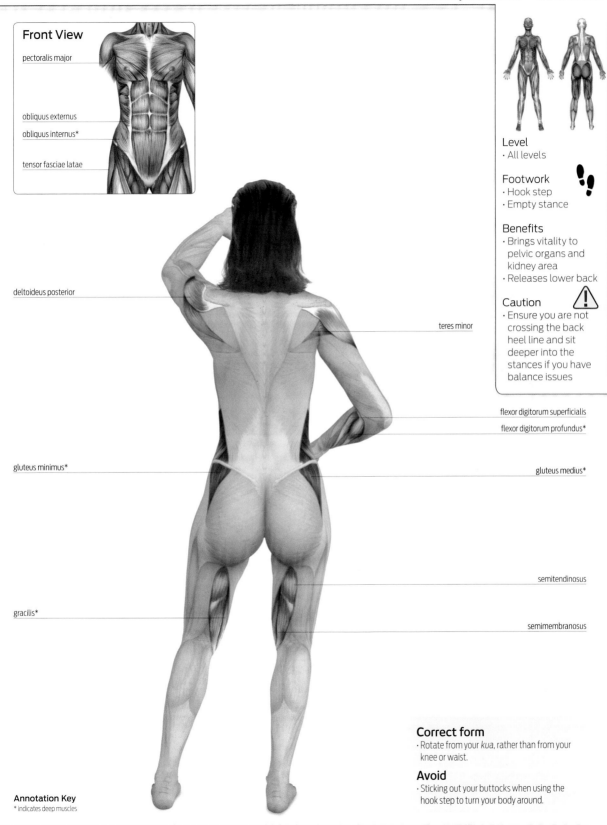

Front View

pectoralis major

obliquus externus

obliquus internus*

tensor fasciae latae

deltoideus posterior

teres minor

flexor digitorum superficialis

flexor digitorum profundus*

gluteus minimus*

gluteus medius*

semitendinosus

gracilis*

semimembranosus

Level
· All levels

Footwork
· Hook step
· Empty stance

Benefits
· Brings vitality to
  pelvic organs and
  kidney area
· Releases lower back

Caution
· Ensure you are not
  crossing the back
  heel line and sit
  deeper into the
  stances if you have
  balance issues

Correct form
· Rotate from your *kua*, rather than from your
  knee or waist.

Avoid
· Sticking out your buttocks when using the
  hook step to turn your body around.

Annotation Key
* indicates deep muscles

Parry and Punch

Parrying gets something out of the way, and punching is a very decisive action. In martial arts, the angle at which you parry, as well as the timing of a punch, makes all the difference to its effectiveness. This posture teaches you to do only the minimum it takes to get something out of the way and then to follow up with determined action. Parry while you are still back-weighted, and use the forward lunging motion to drive a whole-body punch.

1 To perform Parry, rotate your right leg outwardly and turn your torso slightly to the right. Draw in your right elbow to your right hip, while pushing your left arm in front of you and sweeping it up and across to your centerline. Emptily whole step your left foot forward to 9 o'clock, heel first.

2 To perform Punch, shift your weight to your left leg in a bow-and-arrow stance, and punch with your right hand, positioning your left palm near your right inner elbow. Finish the punch with the fist thumb-side up.

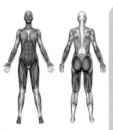

Correct form
· Release all tension in your fist immediately
  after the punch.

Avoid
· Lunging too far forward when you get into
  the bow-and-arrow stance
· Holding your breath. Release your breath as
  you punch, whether fast or slow.

Level
· All levels

Footwork
· Empty step
· Whole step
· Bow-and-arrow
  stance

Benefits
· Creates feeling of
  empowerment
· Increases
  coordination

Caution
· Ensure you are not
  crossing the back
  heel line and sit
  deeper into the
  stances if you have
  balance issues

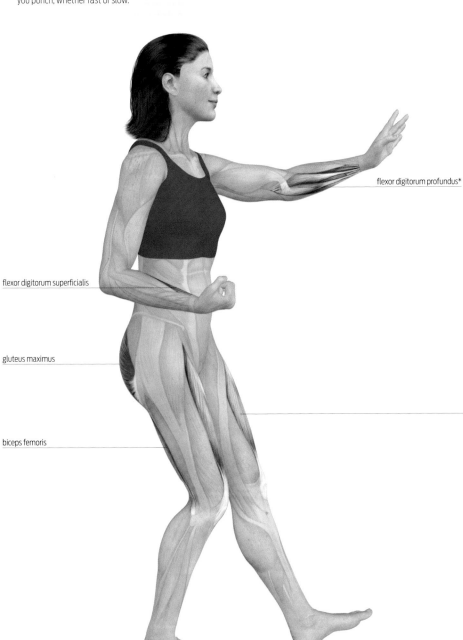

flexor digitorum profundus*

flexor digitorum superficialis

gluteus maximus

biceps femoris

rectus femoris

Annotation Key
* indicates deep muscles

Withdraw and Push

Have you ever watched an ocean wave? After it crashes upon the shore, the water recedes. The water is recycled into the build-up of the next wave's energy as it reaches the land. In the same manner, draw the energy in as you withdraw your leg and arms. Then, like the wave crashing upon the shore, your whole body slowly drives forward as you push. After the push, let up slightly in preparation for the next tai chi posture.

1 Open your fist after performing Punch, and turn up your right palm while crossing your left hand, palm down, under your right upper arm. Shift your weight back onto your right leg while sliding your left hand down your right arm to the wrist, rotating your left palm up as it passes your right elbow.

2 Pull your elbows down to your sides. Face your palms forward as you sink on your right leg, with your left toes pointing up.

3 Flatten your left foot while shifting into a bow-and-arrow stance. While shifting forward, push out your palms, slanting them upward to shoulder height. You are still facing 9 o'clock.

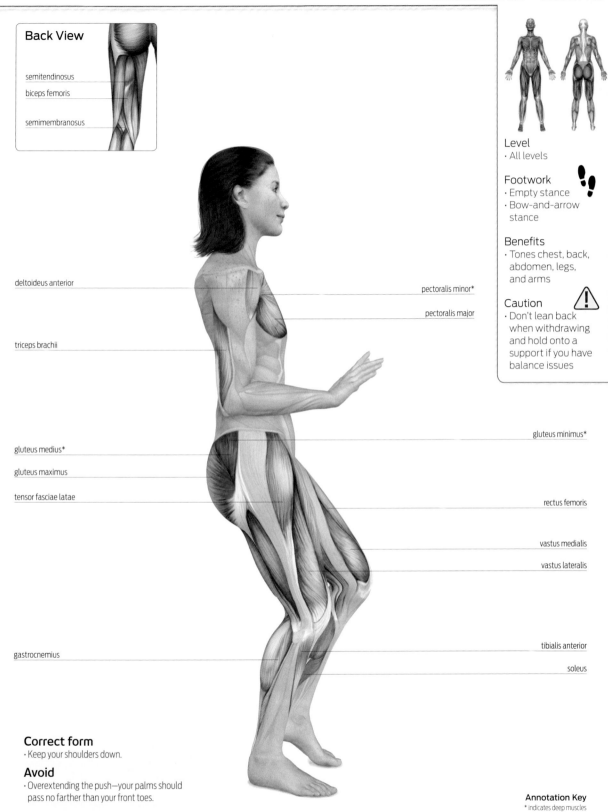

Back View

semitendinosus

biceps femoris

semimembranosus

Level
· All levels

Footwork
· Empty stance
· Bow-and-arrow stance

Benefits
· Tones chest, back, abdomen, legs, and arms

Caution
· Don't lean back when withdrawing and hold onto a support if you have balance issues

deltoideus anterior

pectoralis minor*

pectoralis major

triceps brachii

gluteus minimus*

gluteus medius*

gluteus maximus

tensor fasciae latae

rectus femoris

vastus medialis

vastus lateralis

tibialis anterior

soleus

gastrocnemius

Correct form
· Keep your shoulders down.

Avoid
· Overextending the push—your palms should pass no farther than your front toes.

Annotation Key
* indicates deep muscles

Cross Hands

The traditional Yang 24 Short Form ends with Cross Hands. This posture relieves stress and any built-up tension. Face forward and assume a narrow horse stance. For more of a workout, lower into a deeper, wider horse stance.

1 Shift your weight back onto your right foot. Raise your arms to face level. Hook step your empty left foot in order to point your toes to 12 o'clock. While turning, separate your arms out to the sides at shoulder height, and then shift all your weight back onto your left foot. Step your right foot in slightly and point your toes to 12 o'clock.

2 At the same time, move your arms in front of you to about shoulder height, with your right arm outside your left as you imagine them encircling a large, lightweight sphere. Cross your wrists, palms facing you, and drop your elbows.

3 Rotate your arms so that your palms face outward, and then drop your palms by flexing the wrists. Your left hand will be on top of your right. Separate your arms to your sides, your palms facing the floor, as you sink your body into a slight squat.

4 Slowly raise your body as your arms continue to sink. When you are standing straight, relax your shoulders, arms, hands, legs, pelvis . . . and release your breath.

Correct form
· Keep your back straight throughout this entire tai chi movement.
· Keep your shoulders down and fingers lightly stretched throughout this movement.
· Round your arms while the wrists are crossed.

Avoid
· Letting your arms do all the work—although the focus is on the movement of the arms, let that movement originate from your torso and be supported by your legs.

Upper Arm

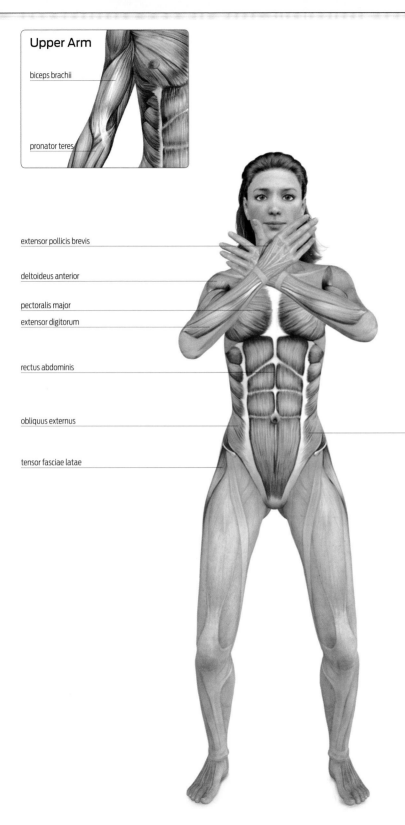

biceps brachii

pronator teres

Annotation Key
* indicates deep muscles

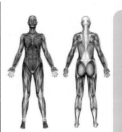

Level
· All levels

Footwork

· Empty stance
· Hook step
· Horse stance

Benefits
· Fosters inner peace
· Promotes hormonal
  and neurological
  balance

Caution
· Safe for most

extensor pollicis brevis

deltoideus anterior

pectoralis major

extensor digitorum

rectus abdominis

obliquus externus

obliquus internus*

tensor fasciae latae

Back View

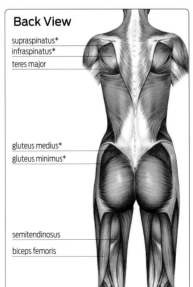

supraspinatus*
infraspinatus*
teres major

gluteus medius*
gluteus minimus*

semitendinosus

biceps femoris

Concluding Posture

End your tai chi chuan practice is with the Closing Posture. Like any other closing posture of tai chi, it releases any residual tension and balances circulation. You can use it alone, before, or after any tai chi meditation or practice.

1 Push your palms down while sinking in your *kua*. As your palms push down, feel the weight in your body sinking and relaxing to the earth. At the same time, feel your neck elongate as the top, back portion of your head pulls toward the sky with your ears in line with your shoulders. Empty your chest as if heaving a sigh of relief or happiness.

2 Draw in your left foot next to your right foot, feet parallel. Let your arms hang down at your sides, all joints relaxed.

3 At the very end, relax everything and stand in peace for a few moments. Breathe deeply and slowly in a calm manner until you feel ready to continue going about your day.

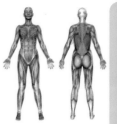

Correct form
· Maintain excellent but relaxed bearing to get maximum benefits from this posture.

Avoid
· Moving quickly—move as slowly as is comfortably possible.

levator scapulae*

deltoideus anterior

pectoralis major

biceps brachii

Level
· All levels

Footwork
· Horse stance

Benefits
· Brings a state of homeostasis and inner peace
· Normalizes blood pressure

Caution
· Safe for most

Back View

trapezius

deltoideus medialis

triceps brachii

latissimus dorsi

erector spinae*

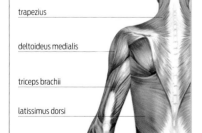

Annotation Key
* indicates deep muscles

Contents

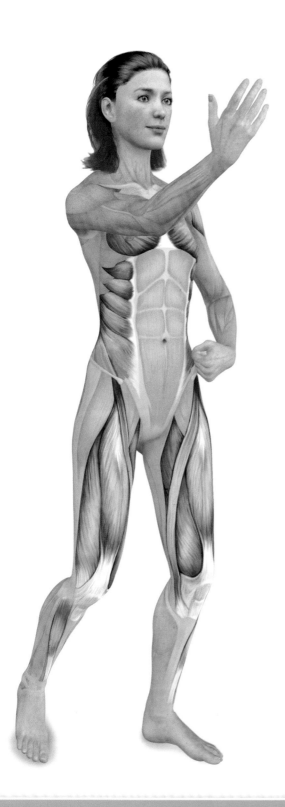

Chen Style

Chen Style is the origin of all the tai chi forms available today. It is known for its ability to restructure the body from the inside out and incorporates more vigorous training than the standard Yang Style so widely practiced today.

Chen Style is said to also rejuvenate and strengthen the sinews, organs, and joints, while heightening the *qi* and spirit. To realize the kind of mastery Chen Style can bestow, one should find a Chen Style master who specifically preserves the traditional approach to tai chi chuan.

Enjoy the following sequence of postures directly excerpted from the traditional Chen New Frame Cannon Fist Form, also known as Chen Second Routine tai chi chuan.

Remember, too, that, like all tai chi chuan, you can alter this form to practice it more slowly, softly, and akin to Yang Style. It is this flexible nature of tai chi chuan that makes it a great regimen for senior citizens or people with injuries and amputations, as well as young athletic men and women. Explore how you can customize it to fit your particular needs and abilities.

Yellow Dragon Stirs Water, Right Side

This posture, from Chen New Frame Cannon Fist, or Chen Second Routine tai chi chuan, develops the body with changes in both translation and rotation in space. While the movement shifts side-to-side, there are a lot of circular, twining movements throughout, which develop the body and its *qi*. This posture sweeps left and right, three times.

1 Step out into a horse stance facing 12 o'clock. Hold your left hand as a fist at your waist and extend your right arm to the side, palm down, fingers stretched.

2 Squat slightly and sweep your right arm in front of you. Shift all your weight to your left leg, slightly rotating your torso to the left, sweeping your arm up to the left, palm up.

3 Begin to slightly rotate your body to face 12 o'clock as you step your right foot out into a horse stance. Simultaneously, rotate your right hand counterclockwise as you sweep your arm in front of your body.

4 Continue shifting your weight to the right, sweeping your arm rightward, rotating slightly to the right, as you end in an empty stance with all weight on the right, palm facing down.

5 Repeat this entire sequence for a total of three times, ending up on the right leg.

Correct form
· Bend deeper in your legs for more of a workout.
· Make the movements higher and the stances narrower if you have knee pain.

Avoid
· Rotating your knees; instead, protect your knees by letting your torso rotate slightly in the hip socket—where rotation belongs.

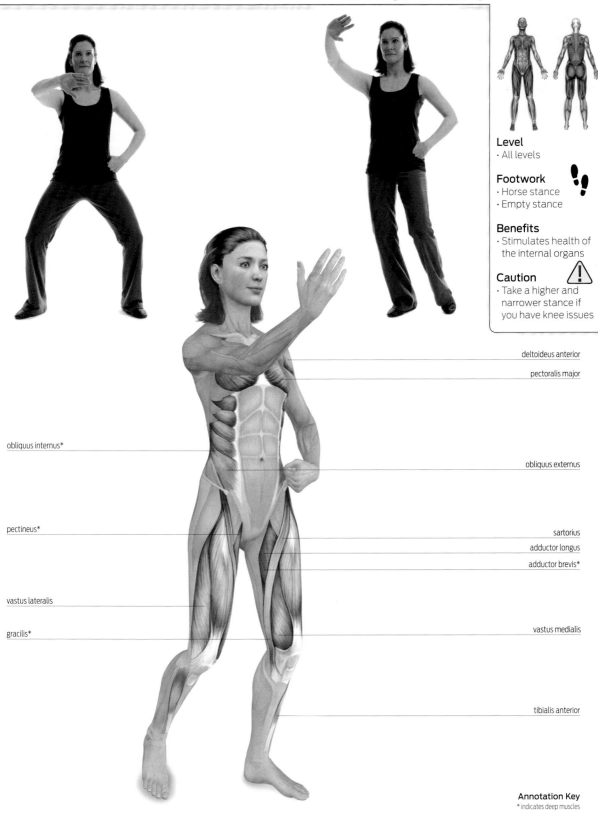

Level
· All levels

Footwork
· Horse stance
· Empty stance

Benefits
· Stimulates health of the internal organs

Caution
· Take a higher and narrower stance if you have knee issues

deltoideus anterior

pectoralis major

obliquus internus*

obliquus externus

pectineus*

sartorius

adductor longus

adductor brevis*

vastus lateralis

gracilis*

vastus medialis

tibialis anterior

Annotation Key
* indicates deep muscles

Yellow Dragon Transition

Each tai chi chuan posture connects to the next by a transition at its endpoint. Transitions often use hook steps or twine steps that help you smoothly change direction. This posture uses a jump, but to turn yourself around you can easily substitute the jump with a series of little hook and twine steps.

1 As you finish the last movement, let your left arm sweep in front of you, and then turn your body clockwise as you jump, so that you face 6 o'clock. To do this, squat, swing both arms down in front of you, jump, and let your arms circle to the left and overhead.

2 As you land, step out in a horse stance, placing your right fist at your waist and your left hand to the side, palm down.

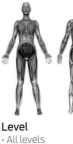

Back View

supraspinatus*
teres minor
teres major

latissimus dorsi

gluteus maximus

infraspinatus*
subscapularis*

triceps brachii

erector spinae*

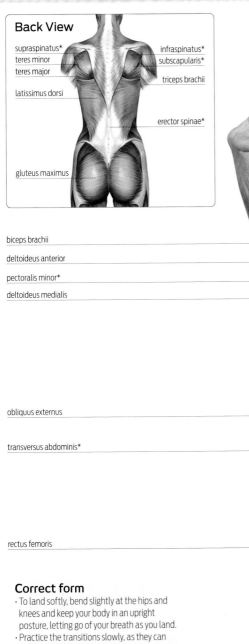

biceps brachii

deltoideus anterior

pectoralis minor*

deltoideus medialis

obliquus externus

transversus abdominis*

rectus femoris

obliquus internus*

gastrocnemius

soleus

Level
· All levels

Footwork
· Hook step
· Twine step

Benefits
· Strengthens bones and cardiovascular system

Caution
· Use a series of twine and hook steps to turn yourself 180 degrees instead of jumping if you have knee issues

Correct form
· To land softly, bend slightly at the hips and knees and keep your body in an upright posture, letting go of your breath as you land.
· Practice the transitions slowly, as they can build your balance and control, thereby enhancing your "muscle memory" so that your body learns to move with grace and power.
· Land with your head and lower back tucked, so that the impact goes *through* your body, instead of *into* your body.

Avoid
· Jumping if you have knee pain or recent surgery or injury—instead, use tight twine steps with your right foot turning outward and hook steps with your left foot turning inward to turn yourself 180 degrees.

Annotation Key
* indicates deep muscles

Yellow Dragon Stirs Water, Left Side

Here you do the mirror image of Yellow Dragon Stirs Water, Right Side. Take notice of how you move your left and right sides of your body—it affords you the perfect opportunity to correct imbalances in your movements. To see muscles not visible in this illustration, simply look at its mirror image on pages 126–127.

1 From the horse stance, squat slightly and sweep your left arm in front of you. Shift all your weight to your right leg, slightly rotating your torso to the right, sweeping your arm up to the right, palm up.

2 Begin to slightly rotate your body to face 6 o'clock again, as you step your left foot out into a horse stance. Simultaneously, rotate your left hand clockwise as you sweep your arm in front.

3 Continue shifting your weight to the left, sweeping your arm leftward, rotating slightly to the left, as you end in an empty stance with all weight on the left, palm facing down.

4 Repeat this entire sequence for a total of three times, ending up on the left leg.

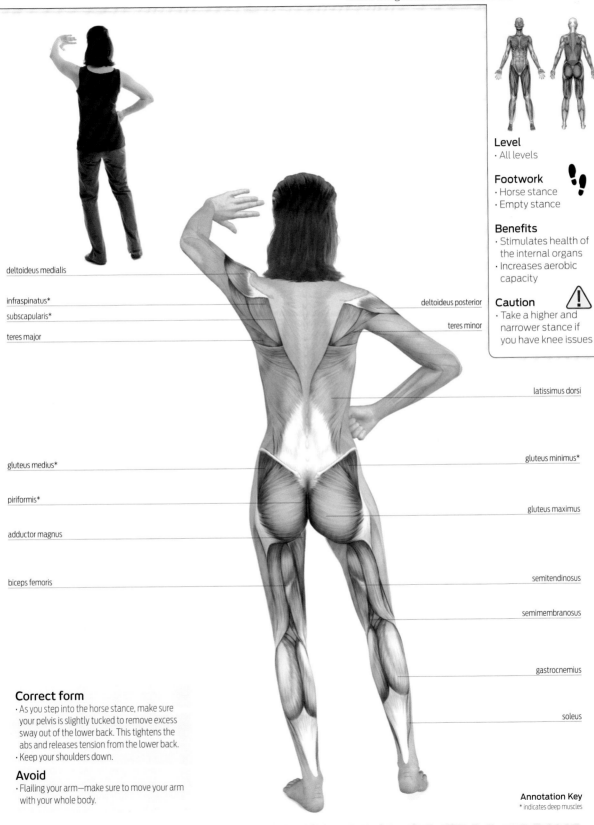

Level
· All levels

Footwork
· Horse stance
· Empty stance

Benefits
· Stimulates health of
  the internal organs
· Increases aerobic
  capacity

Caution
· Take a higher and
  narrower stance if
  you have knee issues

deltoideus medialis

infraspinatus*

subscapularis*

teres major

deltoideus posterior

teres minor

latissimus dorsi

gluteus medius*

piriformis*

adductor magnus

biceps femoris

gluteus minimus*

gluteus maximus

semitendinosus

semimembranosus

gastrocnemius

soleus

Correct form
· As you step into the horse stance, make sure
  your pelvis is slightly tucked to remove excess
  sway out of the lower back. This tightens the
  abs and releases tension from the lower back.
· Keep your shoulders down.

Avoid
· Flailing your arm—make sure to move your arm
  with your whole body.

Annotation Key
* indicates deep muscles

Kick with Left Heel

Kick with Left Heel works your balance and core muscles, along with the leg muscles. Kick out to the side in this posture, pushing through the lower sole of your foot and your heel, and kick only as high as is comfortable.

1 Step your right foot to the right, and pull your left foot in as an empty step with no weight on it. At the same time, cross your left wrist over your right in front of your lower abdomen.

2 Lift your left knee, and raise your arms to a horizontal position in front of you. Kick your left heel out to the side as you thrust out your arms to your sides, hands in fists.

3 After kicking, draw your leg back in, knee up in a rooster stance and draw your arms back inward, in front of you. Release your fists.

Correct form
· If you can't hold your leg out in the kick, just touch your toe down on the floor as lightly as possible, and hold for 5 to 10 seconds. This will help improve your balance.

Avoid
· Holding your breath; instead release your breath to keep pressure out of your chest.
· Raising your shoulders.

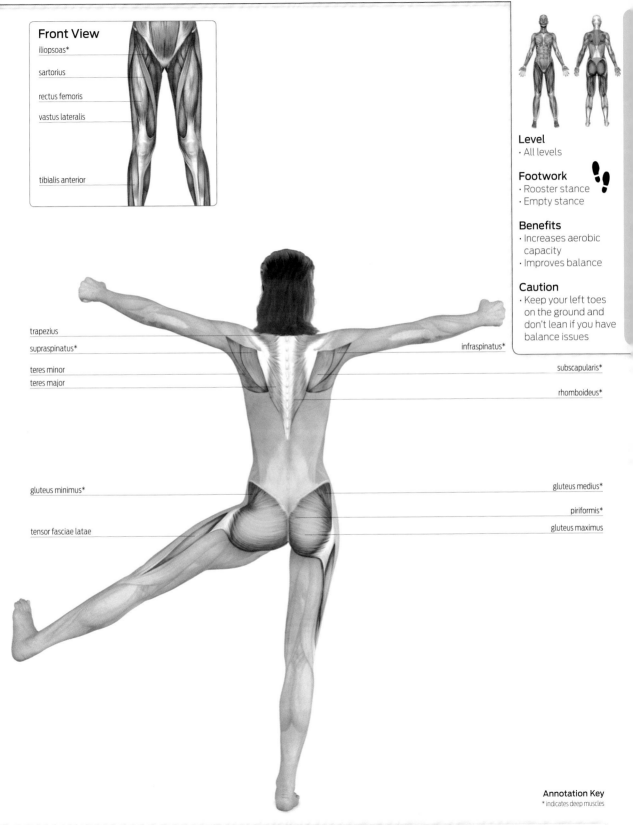

Front View

iliopsoas*

sartorius

rectus femoris

vastus lateralis

tibialis anterior

Level
· All levels

Footwork
· Rooster stance
· Empty stance

Benefits
· Increases aerobic
  capacity
· Improves balance

Caution
· Keep your left toes
  on the ground and
  don't lean if you have
  balance issues

trapezius

supraspinatus*

teres minor

teres major

infraspinatus*

subscapularis*

rhomboideus*

gluteus minimus*

gluteus medius*

piriformis*

tensor fasciae latae

gluteus maximus

Annotation Key
* indicates deep muscles

Kick Transition

The Kick Transition will turn you back to face the front of the room—where you started from in this posture. Feel free to use a spin or series of small hook and twine steps to turn yourself counterclockwise 180 degrees.

1 From the Kick with Left Heel, twine step your left leg by rotating your leg outward and setting your heel down in an empty stance with no weight on it. At the same time, lower yourself a little on your right leg as you turn your torso a bit to the left.

2 Spin, and immediately shift your weight onto your left leg as you turn your body counterclockwise to again face 12 o'clock. Keep your posture very straight as you spin so that you don't lose your balance.

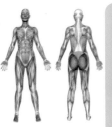

Correct form

· Set your left empty heel down as close to
  your body as possible to make the spin easier
  and tighter.
· If you can't spin with a twine step, use a series
  of left-foot twine steps and right-foot hook
  steps to orient yourself to face 12 o'clock.
· Whenever you kick, sit a little into the stance to
  improve your balance and control.

Avoid

· Leaning your back or head forward. Relax your
  weight down, and keep your back straight, in
  line with the force of gravity.
· Leaning your body forward as you transition,
  which will overload your knees and disrupt
  your balance.

Level
· All levels

Footwork
· Twine step
· Empty stance

Benefits
· Builds fine
  motor skills
· Improves balance

Caution
· Take a higher and
  narrower stance if
  you have knee issues

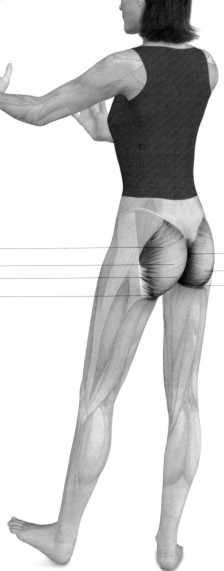

gluteus maximus

obturator internus*

gemellus inferior*

quadratus femoris*

piriformis*

gemellus superior*

obturator externus*

Annotation Key
* indicates deep muscles

Kick with Right Heel

In Kick with Right Heel, you simply perform the mirror image of Kick with Left Heel. Try to equalize the left and right sides of your body as best as possible.

1 From Kick Transition, you will end with your wrists crossed in front of your lower abdomen, right wrist on the outside.

2 Lift your right knee, and raise your arms to a horizontal position in front of you. Kick your right heel out to the side as you thrust out your arms to your sides, hands in fists.

Correct form
· Use gravity to find your balance by aligning your posture with it as best as possible—in a straight line.
· If you can't hold your leg out in the kick, just touch your toe down as lightly on the floor as possible, and hold for 5 to 10 seconds. This will help improve your balance.
· Tighten your fists only at the most outstretched part of the movement.

Avoid
· Tilting your body to the opposite side to counterbalance you as you kick your leg out to the side. Instead, imagine you are sitting down on a high stool.
· Holding your breath; instead release your breath to keep pressure out of your chest.
· Raising your shoulders.

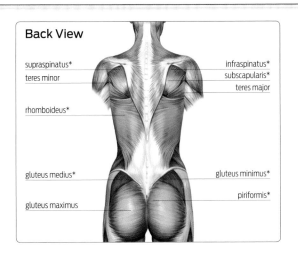

Back View

supraspinatus*
teres minor

infraspinatus*
subscapularis*
teres major

rhomboideus*

gluteus medius*

gluteus minimus*
piriformis*

gluteus maximus

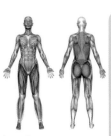

Level
· All levels

Footwork
· Rooster stance
· Empty stance

Benefits
· Increases aerobic capacity
· Improves balance

Caution
· Keep your right toes on the ground and don't lean if you have balance issues

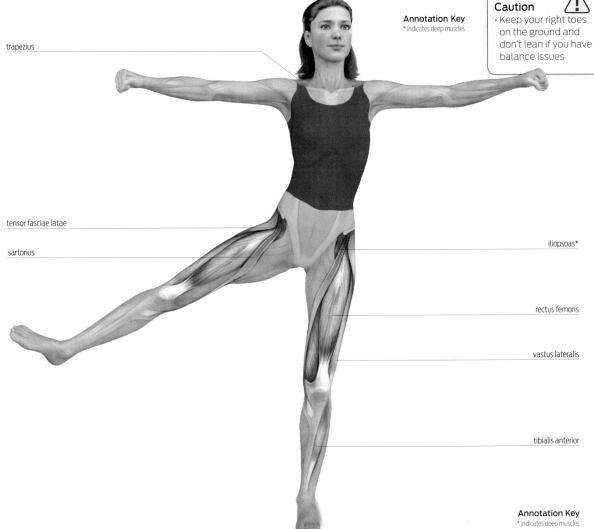

Annotation Key
* indicates deep muscles

trapezius

tensor fasciae latae

sartorius

iliopsoas*

rectus femoris

vastus lateralis

tibialis anterior

Annotation Key
* indicates deep muscles

Turn Up Flowers from Sea Bottom

In Turn Up Flowers from Sea Bottom, a short twist moves you 90 degrees to the right. This posture uses the rooster stance along with two loosely held fists.

1 From Kick with Right Heel, quickly retract your right leg (knee up, foot down) into a rooster stance as you spin 90 degrees clockwise to face 3 o'clock. Spin lightly and quickly on your left leg with your spine straight.

2 At the same time, pull your arms in, ending with your left arm up, hand in a fist at the height of your head, and your right elbow by your right hip, also in a fist, facing palm up.

Correct form
· Retract your arms and leg at the same time the spin occurs to give momentum to the spin.
· Use the momentum of the pulling in of your right leg and arms to help you spin effortlessly.
· Imagine you are sitting down at the end of this tai chi posture.

Avoid
· Holding your fists too tightly; only squeeze them as you are turning through the movement, but then immediately release the tension afterward.
· Spinning if you have knee or foot pain, Instead, use a series of tight twine and hook step movements to gently turn yourself to the right.

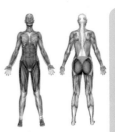

Back View

obturator externus*   obturator internus*

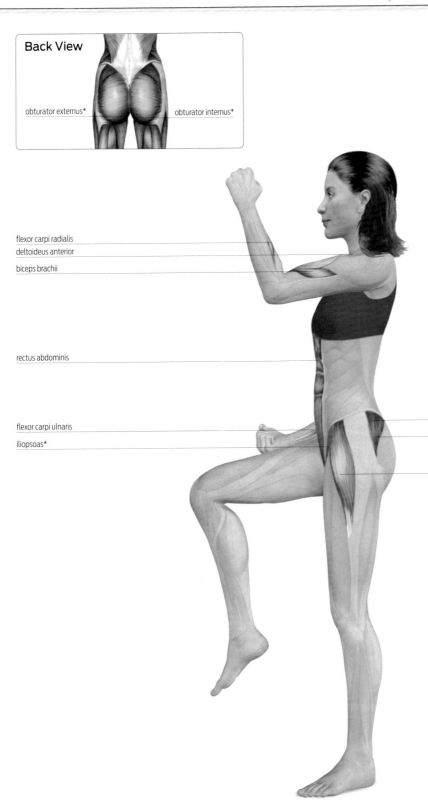

flexor carpi radialis

deltoideus anterior

biceps brachii

rectus abdominis

flexor carpi ulnaris

iliopsoas*

gluteus medius*

gluteus minimus*

tensor fasciae latae

Level
· All levels

Footwork
· Rooster stance

Benefits
· Increases focus, control, and coordination

Caution
· Keep your right toes on the ground, and sink your weight into the stance if you have balance issues

Annotation Key
* indicates deep muscles

Hidden Hand Punch

When executing Hidden Hand Punch, imagine you are punching through something, using your body to power it instead of overextending your arm. To punch properly, keep your wrist straight and your thumb curled over the second segment of your first two fingers.

1 From Turn Up Flowers from Sea Bottom, set your right foot down next to your left as you extend your left leg in front of you on your heel as an empty step. At the same time, extend your left arm in front, palm open. Retract your right hand into a loose fist to your side. Your torso will slightly rotate to the right as a result.

2 Shift your weight forward onto your left leg to power the punch. Slightly rotate your arm inward to give rotation to your fist as you are punching. Your torso will slightly rotate to the left, ending up facing centered. This movement also powers the punch.

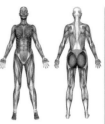

Correct form

· Sit when you hit; in other words, you should
  feel a sense of rooting, sitting, or dropping your
  torso as you approach the imagined impact.
· Keep your elbows facing down. As you punch,
  imagine your arms are like a horizontally
  positioned pulley; as the right goes out, the left
  retracts a little.
· Keep your wrist straight and your thumb curled
  over the outside of your index and middle
  fingers as you make a fist.

Avoid

· Holding continuous tension in a punch.
  Squeeze or tighten your fist only at the
  moment of imagined impact and then
  immediately relax it.
· Holding your breath. Release your breath as
  you punch, whether fast or slow.
· Stretching out the punching arm indefinitely.
  After any punch, relax your arms and let the
  punching arm retract slightly.

Level
· All levels

Footwork
· Bow-and-arrow
  stance
· Empty stance

Benefits
· Builds confidence
· Releases trapped
  emotions

Caution
· Safe for most

deltoideus anterior

pectoralis major

deltoideus posterior

deltoideus medialis

biceps brachii

triceps brachii

serratus anterior

obliquus internus*

obliquus externus

gluteus maximus

Annotation Key
* indicates deep muscles

Closing Posture

Like putting a period at the end of a sentence, perform Closing Posture at the end of any tai chi practice, such as the previous Chen form. Closing Posture gives your body and mind a sense of accomplishment and wholeness, "sealing" the energy and teaching your body to come to a state of relaxation and centeredness. Make sure to fully release your breath and chest, while at the same time keeping your head straight with your ears in line with your shoulders. You can hold this posture for a few meditative minutes.

1 From Hidden Hand Punch, release your fist and step your right foot next to your left, squatting slightly. At the same time, press both palms down toward the earth, arms at your sides, shoulders depressed. Release your breath.

2 Let all excess tension leave your body and mind as you exhale and slowly rise to a tall but relaxed standing position.

Back View

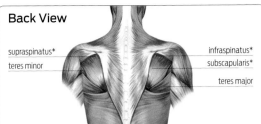

supraspinatus*

teres minor

infraspinatus*

subscapularis*

teres major

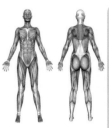

Level
· All levels

Footwork
· Horse stance

Benefits
· Brings focus
  and peace

Caution
· Safe for most

deltoideus posterior

triceps brachii

Correct form

· Imagine that your lower body and shoulders
  are like sacks of heavy sand, weighting into
  the earth, and the top and back area of your
  head is being lifted by a string connected to a
  gigantic helium balloon.
· Keep your head extended to the sky and the
  rest of your body sinking toward the earth.

Avoid

· Moving quickly—move as slowly as is
  comfortably possible in order to get the
  maximum benefits of energy and relaxation.
  You will feel the stress of the world slipping off
  your shoulders and a warm comfortable flow
  of blood and energy circulation.
· Overdoing it. This is a simple, slow, peaceful
  move. Resist the temptation to make it
  dramatic—let it be light and peaceful.

Annotation Key
* indicates deep muscles

Contents

There is much you can do both during your practice and in your everyday life that will enhance your tai chi practice. Learning how to breathe properly and to meditate will relax and rejuvenate you. Employing tai chi's principles of structure will allow you to complete daily chores more easily and more efficiently. Most important, learning to hold and move your body with proper structure will help you deal with existing pain and avoid further injury.

To enhance your tai chi practice, you first need to learn the problems a majority of tai chi practitioners face. The problems are often traceable to just a few root causes; once the root cause is addressed, the problems usually resolve with ease.

Enhancing Tai chi

Breathing methods

Do you have to breathe a special way in tai chi chuan practice? No—but you do have to learn to cultivate your breathing so that you never hold your breath.

Almost everyone is a "breath holder" to some degree. When we concentrate or struggle, whether physically or mentally, we tend to hold our breath. Tai chi chuan practice therefore requires you to pay attention to your breath and take the action to let it go.

Let it go

For hundreds of years, the guides who escort travelers up to high elevations, such as Mount Fuji or the Himalayas, have cautioned their clients to emphasize their exhalations rather than their inhalations to combat altitude sickness caused by oxygen deficit. The more you let go, the more energy you can receive.

Let go by conscientiously relaxing your chest area over and over. Use the sound *hahhhh*, and activate it as though it was a sigh of relief or contentment. In fact, it is said that a sigh is the body's natural way of releasing the breath to allow for better oxygenation and *qi* flow.

Qigong

Specialized breathing exercises have come to be known as "qigong" in China. *Qi* refers to your life-force energy, and *gong* means the skillful work required to cultivate it. There are many qigong exercises and sets, and tai chi chuan is considered to be a sophisticated and powerful type of qigong practice.

To explore the qigong aspects of tai chi chuan, experiment with timing your inhalations and exhalations to the beginning half and ending half of each tai chi posture and transition. Then forget the timing, and just keep draining your chest area, allowing your breathing to become fuller and slower, while expressing in the lower abdomen. You will find with practice that your breathing takes care of itself—an indication that you are receiving the benefit of *qi* cultivation from your tai chi chuan.

Breathing the Square

There are also a few breathing methods that will adjust your energy quite effectively. Breathing the Square, a tai chi breath regulator exercise, is one of the easiest breathing practices with the most outstanding, instantly noticeable effects. Feel free to do this before or after tai chi, meditation, or any time in your daily life. It can help you start your day, and it can help you get to sleep. It's an excellent way to quell anxiety, gain confidence, and reduce chronic pain.

Keeping balance

Various civilizations see the square as a symbol of balance and solidity. "Square breathing," or "breathing the square," is a balancing exercise that also stabilizes your mood, *qi*, and physiological functions. It can rev you up or soothe jangled nerves. It is an excellent energy-based antidote to grief, depression, anger, and anxiety.

Establish a rhythm

If you have a slow piece of relaxing music, you can try to base the counts on the rhythm of that music. If you are in public, such as on a train, listen for the steady beat of some machinery or other sound to guide you. Other people like to use their heartbeat to base the count, or just an intuitive rhythm of their own.

To begin, sit or lie down in a comfortable position. Place your hands comfortably on your lap or on your lower abdomen (dantian). You will be counting as you breathe. You can either count your heartbeats, the ticking of a clock, the rhythmic beat of slow music, or your own arbitrary pace.

First take a big chest breath, expanding your ribs as much as possible, and then, in one fell swoop, let it all out. You will feel your chest relax and sink in. Now, try to maintain that relaxed feeling with your chest drained of excess tension.

From here on, let all your breath movement occur in your lower abdomen—the dantian—trying to reduce the chest activity of breathing as much as possible. Imagine the tension draining off your chest, which also helps to keep tension out of your heart and lungs.

Either close your eyes, or let your vision become relaxed and diffuse. Inhale by expanding your abdomen, and exhale by allowing it to "deflate." Practice this for a few moments at a pace comfortable for you.

Next, inhale for a count of four, gently hold for a count of four, and then exhale for a count of four and hold for a count of four. If a four-count is uncomfortable, start with a count of three.

To develop your relaxation as well as aerobic capacity, simply elongate all your counts to five, then six, and so on.

Dantian compressions and expansions

Though simple in its essence, this is an advanced breathing method done only by those who have learned to free up and "let go" of their breath. This technique is the basis for the advanced Taoist qigong technique called "breathing without breathing." Dantian compressions and expansions may be difficult for beginners, so don't worry—just focus on square breathing and releasing chest air while doing your tai chi.

Once you are able to effortlessly keep your chest and ribs released of breath-holding patterns, you can try the dantian compressions and expansions. All you do is pull in your lower-abdominal muscles as deeply as possible and then expand your abdomen.

Unlike square breathing and deep breathing, during dantian compressions and expansions, you do not concern yourself with matching your inhalations and exhalations to your abdominal movements. You just constantly relax your breath and allow it to occur of its own accord. Your body contains the wisdom to know how and when to inhale and exhale if you keep it aligned and released.

In dantian compressions and expansions, you pull in the front of your dantian (the lower abdominal wall) as though you wanted to pull it to your tailbone.

Keep your breathing free, letting it do what it wants. Then relax, and expand the dantian. Your first inclination may lead you to try expanding your abdomen, but you actually want to expand the rear of your abdominal cavity, pressuring it toward your lower back.

At the same time, imagine two guidewires rooting your energy in place to the earth—one emanating from your dantian to the floor in front of you and one emanating from your lower back to the floor behind you. Relax all your muscles and breathe naturally, and then repeat.

Dantian compressions and expansions are said to build qi and energy, control and cultivate the dantian, and benefit the organs of digestion and the sexual organs. It also grounds your energy and increases both blood and lymphatic circulation. It is imperative that you keep your back straight when you attempt this exercise.

Tai chi in your daily life

Tai chi is more than a set of postures and forms—it is a way of life. Mindfully applying its principles to everyday activities enriches your life as well as your body.

Tai chi is based on the patterns and movements of nature, so why should it remain isolated from your daily life? If you only practice a mindful exercise for a few minutes or hours per day, then what happens with the majority of your day? Wouldn't it be more beneficial to you if you could carry your mind-body exercise benefits into the bulk of your day?

Tai chi's breathing methods, stretching, meditation, and mind-set can all be incorporated into your daily routine. Master Jou Tsung Hwa, a famous tai chi grandmaster, would ask his students to ask this of themselves: "For everything you see, do, and experience, ask yourself, 'How is this like tai chi?'" Yin and yang is part of everything. That is the real truth of tai chi.

Let's take a look at examples of how common activities can be used to give you tai chi benefits.

Vacuuming, sweeping, raking, and mopping

Daily chores, such as pushing a vacuum, broom, rake, or mop, use movements very similar to the Yang Style Push and Roll Back movements of the Grasp Sparrow's Tail posture. Taking a bow-and-arrow stance, use all the same principles that apply to Push. When pulling the object to you, experiment with how this is similar to the Roll Back movement. Breathe with the movement, or practice letting your breathing relax and release.

Picking up and setting down objects

Stooping over and straining is a no-no in tai chi chuan, as it is in daily life. Any time you need to pick up or set down a heavy or unwieldy object, use a wide horse stance with knees placed outward.

Get as close as possible to the object or area you are reaching to. The closer it is situated to your center, the less energy you will waste. Pick up the object or set it down by keeping your buttocks tucked and your elbows and shoulders relaxed downward. Exhale upon the "work" exertion. This also works great when you reach into a closet, cabinet, or refrigerator.

Sitting and standing

Try sitting on a chair by taking a wider horse stance and lowering yourself straight down, instead of stooping over in an attempt to park your derriere on it. To rise from the chair, align your spine, keep your knees outward over your toes, and imagine someone is hoisting you up from your *kua* area.

Dealing with tense situations

Whether it is a minor stressor, such as that rude sales clerk or an endless line at the supermarket, or a major ordeal, when you feel yourself getting tense from an annoying or upsetting situation, try to see it fading out of you instead of remaining stuck inside you. Take a moment and relax your weight down, lower your breathing, and then mindfully and peacefully proceed to deal with the situation. This practice cultivates the wise demeanor of the ancient tai chi masters.

When you truly get the feeling and wisdom of tai chi, you will realize that you don't do tai chi—you become it. Then, more and more positive energy will enter your body and your life.

What do you do when you meditate?

Contrary to popular belief, you are not just "doing nothing" when you meditate. The most effective method is to observe what is going on in your mind and body. Don't get involved with what you observe; don't judge it. Pretend you are watching what's going in inside of you, as if watching a TV program. Notice the physical feelings of your body and what you are thinking about them. Are you happy? Irritated? Confused? At peace? What emotions surface? Observe them and then let them float away. What is going on in your body? Are you clenching a muscle somewhere that you can unclench? Can you imagine tension melting out? When you relax, are you slipping into bad posture again? Repeatedly doing this will bring balance back to your mind and body.

Meditation

Meditating is one of the most calming things you can do to enhance your daily life. For tai chi, meditation heightens your awareness of your body and your ability to control it. It also enhances your ability to release stress and relax. In advanced and esoteric practices of tai chi, meditation increases your *qi* and other intrinsic mental and physical abilities.

Sitting meditation

This is the easiest form of meditation and the best choice for beginners. Sitting meditation also strengthens your back and aligns your spine.

Find a comfortable but firm chair or sit cross-legged on a yoga mat or blanket. Make sure your head is pulled in so that your ears are in line with your shoulders. Lift the top, back portion of your head to the sky so that you have a slight traction on your cervical spine. Allow your shoulders to melt downward with gravity. Allow your breathing to become deep, relaxed abdominal breathing. You can close your eyes or leave them open.

Just as important as your upper-body posture is your lower-body posture. Reduce excess sway in your lower back by allowing your pelvis to gently tuck under. Excess sway can lead to tension in the chest and back, which may produce anxiety or nausea. Simply straightening and aligning your posture can eliminate this problem.

If you meditate in a chair, sit on the edge to allow for postural alignment. If sitting on the floor, raise the base of your spine by placing a cushion or folded blanket underneath you. This fosters proper alignment and reduces tension in the back and pelvic muscles.

Calm down

Here's a trick to calm your mind if it races wildly: Ask yourself over and over, "What is my next thought going to be?" Before you can answer it, ask that question again.

Standing meditation

Standing meditation allows you to reap the benefits of meditation at any time. Use the same straight posture, relaxed breathing, and techniques of sitting meditation, but instead, stand. Standing meditation practice is mandatory for development and progress in all the traditional practices of tai chi chuan. In time, you can develop incredible structural and energetic powers that can augment martial skills and foster enlightenment.

To begin, stand in either a narrow or deep horse stance. You can also experiment with the bow-and-arrow stance, or use tai chi postures for standing meditation.

As you get more comfortable, take wider and deeper stances and hold them for longer amounts of time.

Your goal is to tell yourself to relax into the work and tension of holding deeper and deeper stances. This will re-train your mind and body to immediately respond with relaxation in times of stress, instead of responding with the usual reflex of prolonged tension and struggle.

Wait at least 30 minutes before or after eating before meditating. You can precede or conclude your meditation session with the Breathing the Square exercise if desired. If you experience unusual mental or physical discomfort, simply end the session.

Tai chi troubleshooting

Addressing structural imbalances is the best way to troubleshoot your tai chi practice. There are numerous simple steps you can take to avoid injury and alleviate pain.

earn to troubleshoot structural issues before they become major problems. Most problems and pain during and after tai chi chuan practice can be traced to faults in structure, which can be in the upper body, lower body, or both.

Upper-body problems usually arise when the head is not sitting correctly atop the spine. Your ears must be in line with your shoulders, and your chin should be level with the ground. You do not need to pull your shoulders back hard, but you must "drain" and relax your chest inwardly to drop tension and improve your balance.

Problems in the lower body include excess sway in the lower back, leaning backward in an attempt to correct a sway back, stooping forward, hiking one hip higher than the other, turning the torso in the knees instead of the *kua*, crossing the back heel line, not releasing weight off one leg when employing twist steps or hook steps, and allowing the front knee or both knees to buckle inward. Holding the abdomen in instead of just tucking the pelvis under blocks the dantian and *qi* energy.

Check the table below for a quick guide to solving common issues that may impede your tai chi practice.

Problem	Solution
Knee pain	Your knee might be buckling in on certain stances, so use higher and narrower stances, and make sure your buttocks are not sticking out. Keep your knees in line with your toes. Immediately ice your knees for 10 minutes after practice. If you wear orthotics, ask your doctor about how to wear them for tai chi practice. For further information, explore pages 158-159.
Insufficient body rotation during hook or twine steps	If your hips are tight, their rotation will be limited. Just use a series of small, narrow hook and twine steps to turn your body in the direction you want to go. Remember: where you point your toes is where you centerline goes.
Twist steps feel awkward	Keep the weighted leg very stable, and avoid shifting off the weighted front leg when finishing the twist. Make sure you are not crossing your back heel line, which makes twist steps impossible. Most of all, practice. It's normal for beginners to feel awkward when executing a twist step.
Poor balance	Hold onto sturdy furniture, a walker, or a wall, and then try to let go for a few seconds. Gradually increasing the time you stand without support will improve your balance.
Lack of coordination	Slow down. Consider using washable cosmetics or a dry-erase marker to mark your left and right hands with an L and an R. Remember that tai chi builds coordination—as a beginner, you are not required to already possess it. Be more patient with yourself.
Shortness of breath	A sway back pushes out the chest and blocks breathing. Relax your chest inward by saying *hahhhh* often—as if you were breathing a sigh of relief. It will relax your shoulders downward as well. Go slow, and break your practice time up instead of doing it in one long session. Study pages 146-147.
Memory difficulties	Spend more time repeating just a few moves over and over. Tai chi is excellent for boosting the memory. Pay more focused attention to what you are doing. Say the movements aloud as you are doing them—this improves your problem-solving skills as a by-product. Consider keeping a tai chi journal to record your notes.
Trouble releasing tension	Gently rock and shake your body at the end of each tai chi posture, as you would shake water off your hands. Let your breath out as you do this. Feel your weight dropping, muscles and joints loosening, and tension dropping off you to the earth. Traditional tai chi masters employ the shaking technique for their own practice.
Hand or leg tremors	Shaking or tremors is common in cases of nerve damage, multiple sclerosis, Parkinson's disease, and other neurological conditions. Review pages 40–41, and do the stretching *qi* down to the belly of the fingers exercise. You can also perform the same exercise with your leg, starting from the dantian and hips, stretching the *qi* down to the bottom of the foot.
Inability to sleep after nighttime practice	Make sure to avoid eating a heavy meal at least 30 minutes before practice. Slow your practice down and consider doing the Yang Style tai chi chuan at night. Turn the lights down low, as this helps adjust your melatonin levels for optimal sleep. Avoid computers, televisions, mobile phones, and other distractions right after tai chi practice and before bedtime.
Other problems/ stiffness or pain	Explore the various tai chi remedial exercises within this section. If pain or health problems persist, please consult your doctor.

Stay positive

If you spot one of your problems in the table opposite, take extra time to examine the situation. We sometimes think we are not making an error, when indeed we are. When you do find an error—work on correcting it. Be sure, however, to balance this endeavor with finding something that you are doing right or in which you are making progress, no matter how minimal. Positive reinforcement will help you enhance your tai chi practice.

Hand and wrist flexibility

Tai chi is excellent for the health of the wrists and hands. Several medical studies have demonstrated tai chi's efficacy in treating arthritis. To boost up the healing power of tai chi, be certain to always stretch the trapped shoulder energy down the arms and out the bellies of the fingers. Don't just stretch it to the forearms—make sure it stretches all the way out through the fingers.

Grasp the fingers-area only with your other hand, and pull back to stretch, making sure that the wrist is extended back too. Drop your shoulders. Hold the stretch from 30 seconds up to a few minutes.

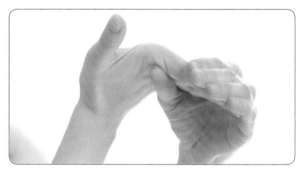

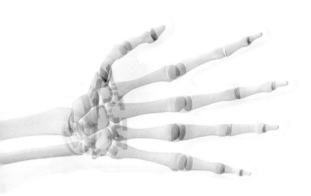

The fingers are hinge joints, but the thumb is a saddle joint, which allows for flexion, extension, adduction, abduction, and circumduction. It needs to be stretched separately.

Slide your fingers over your thumb, and gently pull back and a little out to the side. Keep your shoulders down, breathe, and hold from 30 seconds up to a few minutes.

You can do various stretches to regain or preserve the youthfulness of your wrists and hands. These stretches are perfect for those who spend time working with their hands or typing. It would also benefit those whose careers rely on fine motor skills, such as surgeons, craftspersons, body workers, musicians, and artists.

Release, and then wiggle and flex your fingers and shake out your hand. Repeat both stretches on the fingers and thumb of the other hand.

Notice that if you just let your hands hang loosely, your fingers tend to curl in. This is because the muscles responsible for curling your fingers and flexing your wrist— your wrist flexors—are more powerful than the muscles that straighten your fingers, pull them back, and extend the wrist—your wrist extensors. This can lead to muscle imbalance and joint wear. Regularly stretch out the flexors to preserve your hands and increase circulation.

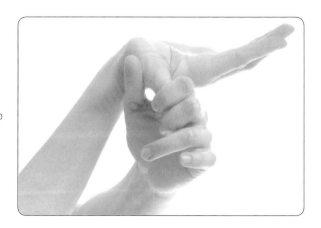

Hand and Wrist Flexor Release

To stretch the flexors of your hand and wrist, hold your arm in front of you, palm facing you, elbow down. You may find it comfortable to lean your elbow against your ribs as you stretch your hands.

Neck stiffness

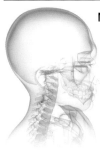

Our daily activities take place predominantly in front of us—when we drive, read, walk, type, we are looking ahead, and by nature our bodies follow where we are looking. This reflex pulls the head forward, something it was not meant to do. The result is that the majority of us exhibit head protraction, which becomes even more pronounced as we age.

The cervical vertebrae of the neck are the smallest, most mobile, and most delicate bones of the spine. Numerous nerve roots branch out from the cervical vertebrae into the peripheral nervous system. Misalignment can compress these nerve roots and cause tingling and malfunction in the upper limbs.

Injury to the neck is common and can cause excruciating pain, leading to headache and depression. To avoid injury, do not allow your head to punish your neck by hanging forward—its joints and muscles receive enough abuse just from daily living.

Although this sign of aging is one of the easiest to correct, very few people make the conscientious choice to correct it. Not only would they function better, feel better, and reverse that particular sign of aging, but they would also be far more attractive too. Nothing looks worse than the aged and defeated silhouette of a head bowed forward. All you need to do is continuously pull your head back so that your ears line up with your shoulders. Do not tip your chin up—no one can walk around with their eyes up in the clouds. Keep your chin level with the ground. This also seats your trachea and thyroid into their proper anatomical positions.

Use the following exercise to release pain and stiffness from your neck. It will make it easier for you to attain and maintain proper alignment. Do not perform this stretch if you have bad pain or were medically advised against this kind of position.

Stay loose

Most neck pain and stiffness isn't serious, but it can limit your abilities and compromise your range of motion. Keep your neck limber to get the most from your tai chi practice.

Cervical Stretch

Sit or stand with straight posture. Keep your shoulders down and your chest relaxed inwardly.

Inhale, and then slightly tip your head back as you exhale. Close your eyes, and let your mouth drop open slightly. Hold for up to 30 seconds, breathing naturally.

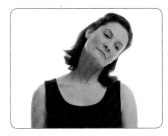

Next, slowly and passively roll your head to the left so that it hovers above your left shoulder. Practice letting go and relaxing your breath. Make sure both of your shoulders are gently pressed down. Hold for 30 to 60 seconds.

Slowly and passively roll your head in front of you so that the bottom of your chin and lower jaw sink toward your upper chest. Breathe, relax, and hold for 30 to 60 seconds.

Slowly and passively roll your head to your right shoulder, again relaxing at this position for 30 to 60 seconds. Repeat tipping your head back as before.

Once you complete this full clockwise cycle, repeat moving in the counterclockwise direction. Repeat the full

Check your range

The Dead Bug gets it name from the way dead beetles lie on their backs with their feet up in the air. However comical its name, its offers an intense workout that will leave you feeling very much alive and invigorated. Unlike the dead beetles, you must keep your four limbs straight and full of *qi* when doing this exercise.

cycle up to three times.

Strengthening your core

Why is the core so important? The core comprises a system of muscles in the lower-trunk area, including the lower back, abdomen, and hips. Working together, these muscles support your entire body—all bodily movement originates through them.

Your core muscles stabilize the trunk and pelvis, allowing your arms and legs to move properly during any activity, including your tai chi practice. Neglecting these muscles can compromise your posture, which often results in a predisposition to injury. A strong core forms a supportive natural corset for your trunk.

Dead Bug

Core exercises abound, but the Dead Bug is a powerful tai chi core conditioner. Various lineages of kung fu also feature similar exercises, which can also be blended with other breathing and mental exercises.

To start, you need a firm surface, but you must add some sort of padding to any hard floor. Carpeting with sufficient padding underneath should suffice, but you may also want to use a yoga mat, throw rug, or folded-up blanket underneath your back to protect your spine. If you have had recent surgery or injury, please consult your doctor before attempting this exercise.

Lie down on the floor face up, making sure to tuck your lower back. Also tuck your chin in so that the back of your head rests fully upon the floor. Take a few moments to relax your body and your breathing.

When you are ready, bend your knees and draw them toward your chest. Then extend your legs straight up into the air, relaxing your feet but still aiming energy out toward the

ceiling. Stretch your legs as high as possible, ideally extending them straight up to form a 90-degree angle with your trunk. If your hamstrings are tight or shortened, you won't be able to extend straight, so try the Biceps Femoris Release (page 160). It is fine, however, to just stretch your legs as high up you are able.

Next, stretch your arms and fingers straight up, pointing to the ceiling. Relax your chest and neck, resisting the tendency to pull up from the floor.

Keep your breath relaxed. Outwardly rotate your arms and legs as much as possible. Rotate from the shoulder blades and shoulder sockets, as well as the hips and the pelvis. It is imperative that you stretch the feeling of *qi* through the limbs the whole time. This will keep them straight. Then rotate them inwardly as much as possible. Stretch intensively through all your limbs.

Repeat for a minimum of five times, making sure to keep your neck and lower back sunk and your breath released.

To release this exercise upon completion, slowly draw your knees to your chest, then roll to your side and gently rise from the floor.

Advance the exercise

For even more advanced development, accompany the limb rotations of this exercise with dantian compressions and expansions. With fully released breath, pull in the dantian upon the outward rotation, and expand the dantian with the inward rotation.

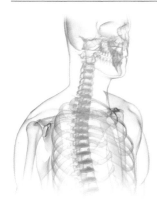

Upper-back and shoulder stiffness

The upper-back and shoulder area is a natural "energy trap" of the human body. All of us have the propensity to hold tension in the shoulders. When the tension gets extreme, it is easy to feel fatigued and irritated. Fatigue and stress will trap further tension into this area of the body—and the cycle goes on and on.

The following exercises will help you "untrap" the energy stored in this area. Perform them slowly, being mindful to exhale through the tension.

Upper-Back Release

This exercise can be as effective as receiving a massage. After completing the moves, it is not uncommon to hear your vertebrae "crack" back into proper alignment.

To begin, sit or stand with straight posture. If sitting, sit on the forward edge of an armless chair or stool. Press your

shoulders down, and aim the energy out the belly of the fingers. Feel as if the top back of your head is being lifted upward, attached to a large helium balloon.

Next, roll your shoulders forward, as if trying to squeeze them together in front of you. This compresses the chest and opens the upper back. Cross your arms at shoulder height while stretching the shoulders out the belly of the fingers to accentuate the stretch.

Let your arms drop and remain completely limp as your raise your shoulders as high as you can until you feel a little pull near the sides of your waist. Then drop your shoulders as you roll them behind you, squeezing hard between the scapulae (shoulder blades).

To accentuate this movement, extend you arms straight behind you and lift them upward while stretching through the belly of the fingers. Retract your head so that your ears are lined up with your shoulders. Remove excess sway from your back. You may lean slightly forward at the front of your hips to help you.

Finally, roll your shoulders down back to your starting position. Repeat in the other direction, for a total of three repetitions on each side.

Shoulder Release

This rotational exercise frees up the shoulder joint and rotator cuff. Another benefit is that it encourages good blood circulation and lymph drainage. It can also help you alleviate fatigue. It's an excellent exercise to do upon awakening and getting ready for your day.

If you had prior rotator cuff injury, move extra slowly, using a smaller range of motion. You should hold each position for a total of 30 to 60 seconds each.

Stay mindful of good structure—keep your head and lower back properly aligned, and remember to breathe. Whenever you feel tension or pain, pause and exhale through it before continuing.

To begin, sit or stand with straight posture. If sitting, perch on the forward edge of an armless chair or stool so that your arms have room to move. Press your shoulders down and aim the energy out the belly of the fingers. This will free up the blocked *qi*.

Feel as if the top back of your head is being tractioned upward, attached to a large helium balloon. Press your shoulder energy down through the belly of the fingers. Then raise your arms in front of you at chest height.

Sit up straight

Poor posture contributes to stiffness and aches in your upper back and shoulders. Be sure to stay mindful of your spinal positioning, whether you are practicing tai chi or just sitting in a chair.

Again, aim the stretch and energy from your shoulders out through the belly of the fingers.

While keeping your upper arms close to your head, raise your arms straight up, again stretching from your shoulder to the belly of the fingers.

Next, rotate your arms behind you. They will naturally spread out a bit to the sides, but reach behind as much as you can. Then press your shoulders down, resuming the same position as when you started.

Repeat the entire exercise in the opposite direction. Perform three repetitions each, circling forward and then backwards.

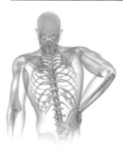

Lower-back stiffness

Our lower backs receive a lot of strain, and a vast majority of adults experience lower-back pain and stiffness at some point in their lives.

Taking time to work the lower-back muscles to keep them limber and mobile increases strength and improves flexibility, which may help prevent future injury.

bloated tummy, but merely gently rolling under the pelvis puts the organs back into proper position in the pelvis—and make you appear as if you lost 10 pounds. A swayed back can also push excess tension and *qi* into the chest, thereby leading to anxiety and possible hypertension.

Improper lifting of heavy objects, or stooping over for tasks that are better accomplished by squatting can also lead to lower-back pain and stiffness. Injury is a leading cause too. If you have had surgery or injury to your lower back, consult with your doctor before attempting this exercise.

Lower-back pain and stiffness can result in either a immobile lower back area or a sway back. Pregnancy often leaves women with a sway back, as does the regular wearing of high heels. A sway back often gives the illusion of having a

Get moving

The lumbar muscles of the lower-back weaken easily, and a sedentary lifestyle does nothing to keep your back strong and healthy. Tai chi gets you moving in a gentle, low-impact regimen that will promote a strong back and a limber body.

Lower-Back Release

The key to doing this exercise properly is to make a "shelf bracket" for your body whenever you find yourself leaning back. This distributes your body weight properly and avoids strain. Accomplish this by placing your hands alongside your spine at the lowest area of your lower back, where it meets the crest of your pelvis. Press in on the muscles and tendons with your fingers or thumbs for extra deep-tissue release.

To begin, sit or stand with straight posture. If sitting, sit on the forward edge of an armless chair or stool so that you have room to move. If standing, use a wide horse stance, and keep both knees bent throughout the exercise.

Inhale, and then exhale as you lean back, making your shelf bracket. Then roll your torso to the left. You can lean your left forearm on your left thigh for extra support. Lean sideways from your waist and hips. Hold this position for 30 to 60 seconds as you breathe, and then relax.

Next, roll your body forward. Lean down as far as possible if you are comfortable. Hold this position for 30 to 60 seconds.

Keeping your knees bent, tip your pelvis under as you slightly lift your upper body upright. Roll to your right, supporting your right forearm on your right leg if desired. Hold this position for 30 to 60 seconds.

Make the shelf bracket, and lean back again, and then rotate in the opposite direction.

Repeat each clockwise and counterclockwise set of rotations for a total of three times.

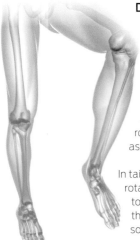

Dealing with knee pain

Knee pain is a common human complaint. The knee is a sensitive joint. It is anatomically classified as a hinge joint, which allows movement in only one direction. The knee does have a very slight ability for lateral and medial rotation, but it often gets misused as if it were a ball-and-socket joint.

In tai chi, as in any activity, keep rotation out of your knee. Any leg or torso rotation belongs in the *kua*—the hip joints. The hip is a ball-and-socket joint designed to withstand a great deal of rotation.

Tai chi should never injure your knees. If you do tai chi and suffer knee pain, your alignment is off or your stances are too low and wide for your current condition. Keeping in line with traditional tai chi principles has helped the knee pain and injuries of millions of people over hundreds of years. The exercises below will also strengthen the knee.

Friction the Knees

You can do this incredibly simple yet incredibly effective exercise this just about any time. Whichever knee you wish to address, extend that leg out in front and a little to the side as an empty stance on the heel. Lock out the knee so your leg is stiff. To "friction," use the edges and heels of your hands to vigorously stroke back and forth beside the kneecap. Then friction above, below, and a little farther out to the sides. The friction should be deep and vigorous but should never cause pain.

Repeat on each knee for a minute or more. Then stand up straight, bend the knee, retract the leg, and walk around for a few moments to reset the muscles and stretch receptors.

Work on your form

Beginners often experience knee pain or stiffness when they first begin their tai chi practice. Some of the more common reasons relate to improper positioning, such as tilting your front knee inward in the postures instead of keeping it vertical. Stay mindful of how you move until proper form becomes second nature.

Adductor Stretch

The muscles that run from your groin area along the inside of your thigh to your knee area are known collectively as the "adductors." Adductors shorten very quickly; they begin to tighten and shrink by your twenties. Tight adductors can pull your knee inward—evidenced by the slight buckling of the front knee readily observed in a long bow-and-arrow stance. This misalignment begins the wear-and-tear of the knee joint. This sign of aging is very easy to reverse, though.

To stretch your adductors, sit on the floor with your legs spread as far apart as you can hold them in a straddle stretch. If you have back pain, sit on a folded-up towel or blanket to elevate your spine.

Pull your spine as straight as possible. You can place your hands on the floor behind you to help push you into straight posture. Tuck your pelvis to eradicate any excess sway in the lower back.

Next, twist your torso to the left leg, inhale, and slowly descend as you exhale. Completely relax your neck muscles, and relax your arms, instead of straining to extend them out. Simply allow gravity to pull the centerline of your torso a little closer to your thigh. Pause and relax for about 30 to 60 seconds.

Now very slowly, rise up. Face the center of your straddle. Inhale, and descend forward, keeping your forearms very close to you on the ground so that you can gently rest your weight on them. Hold 30 to 60 seconds, and then rise.

Repeat the movement to your right thigh, and then come back to a sitting position. You may repeat all steps of this exercise three times. To get up, pull your legs together, lean back on your hands to relax your back, and then draw your knees in, roll to your side, and gently rise.

Keep it steady

Don't worry if you can barely pull your legs apart when you first attempt this stretch—this is all the more reason why you should address this problem now. Never bounce your legs more widely open—you want to feel the stretch in your adductor muscles, but never pain.

Keeping your legs limber and strong

Tai chi calls for you to stay on your feet, and strong legs are essential. Keeping the muscles of your thighs and calves toned and limber will allow you move with grace and agility as you perform the tai chi postures.

Upper-leg stiffness

The muscles of the upper leg, the quadriceps and hamstrings, work as agonists and protagonists to control leg movement. Both groups have attachments to the pelvis, which is part of the body's core. As such, tightness in these muscles can pull on the pelvis in an imbalanced manner, resulting in postural defects. Stretch these muscles on a regular basis, not just to remove stiffness, but also to maintain a healthy body.

Quadriceps Release

Do this exercise standing. Feel free to hold onto a chair or other sturdy object to aid your balance. If you cannot reach and hold your ankle, simply sling a soft belt or cord around your ankle, running the cord up your back, over your shoulder and gripping it to pull it down with your hand.

Stand straight, and then bend your knee and hold your ankle, shoe, edge of shoe, back of your pants, or whatever area you are able to grab. Pull your heel toward your buttocks. As you do this, make sure to touch your inner thighs together. Your knees must be in alignment with each other. If your knee or thigh slips forward, you will not realize the benefit of the stretch.

As you pull your knee toward your buttocks, rock your pelvis under to accentuate the stretch. When done properly, you should feel the stretch along the entire length of the front of your thigh.

Are you breathing? Be sure to exhale, relax your chest, and melt into the intensity of the stretch.

The muscles of your thighs

The great extensor muscles of the knee, the quadriceps femoris, is the large muscle group that covers the front and sides of the femur bone in your upper thigh. Usually referred to as just the "quadriceps" or "quads," this group is made up of four muscles, or "heads." The rectus femoris, located in middle of the thigh, covers most of the other three quadriceps muscles—the vastus lateralis, vastus medialis, and vastus intermedius. Three posterior muscles—the semitendinosus, semimembranosus, and biceps femoris—along with their corresponding tendons, make up the hamstring group. The hamstrings get a lot of work, coming into play during many of our daily activities, such as walking and running.

Biceps Femoris Release

This stretch can be done sitting upon the floor with legs extended out in front of you, or standing, as is shown here.

Begin the stretch by reaching up as high as you can, keeping your forearms near your ears. Stretch your fingers too. Inhale, and then exhale as you stretch down toward your legs. Keep your legs straight but don't lock your knees. Exhale, and relax, feeling the back of your legs release. You may feel a gentle stretch in your lower back as well.

Hold for 30 to 60 seconds. To rise, squat down as you roll your pelvis under in order to tip your torso to a more upright position. Continue slowly rising up.

The Achilles tendon

The stretches below also release the Achilles tendon, the largest and most vulnerable tendon in the human body. Running from the heel to lower calf, it joins the gastrocnemius and soleus to the heel of the foot. While strong, it is not very flexible—stretching it beyond its capacity can result in injuries, such as inflammation, ruptures, and tears.

Lower-leg and ankle flexibility

The largest muscle of the lower leg is the calf muscle, or gastrocnemius. The name means "stomach of the leg," in tribute to its large, bulging shape.

Beneath the gastrocnemius is the soleus muscle. The soleus is often referred to as the "second heart" of the body for its role in pumping back the venous blood to the heart.

The arteries possess muscular walls to help propel along the oxygenated blood in the body, but the veins lack a muscular wall. The job of the veins is to move the oxygen-deprived blood back to the heart. Because the veins have no muscular wall, the only way they can return blood back to the heart is by your movement.

Because tai chi involves more dynamic movement than other mind-body exercises, it is excellent for effectively regulating blood circulation, as well as preventing blood from pooling in the veins. If you keep your lower leg stretched, you are also helping to keep your second heart—the soleus—in good working order.

Calf Release

To begin, assume the longest bow-and-arrow stance that you can. If necessary, hold onto a chair or other sturdy object to balance you. For this exercise, it is permissible to lean a bit forward while holding onto the support object.

Next, extend your back leg even farther, so that your heel starts to come off the floor. Inhale, and then slowly and gently attempt to press your back heel to the floor as you exhale. Straightening your knee will accentuate the stretch. Do not bounce—just breathe and hold for up to 60 seconds.

Relax your foot, bring your leg in, and repeat on the other side. Repeat three or more times on each leg.

Contents

The Tai Chi Challenge will help you power up your tai chi practice. If you have rushed through the book to reach this section, however, you will not attain real progress. Challenge yourself only after consistent practice of the basics, which will establish a strong foundation.

After trying a few of these exercises and variations, brainstorm other ways to challenge yourself. Avoid entertaining the idea that tai chi must feel like strain or struggle to attain any benefit. Learn to relax into its intensity without softening your tai chi practice so much that it becomes a lackadaisical excuse of an exercise regimen. Strive for balance in your mind, body, and life.

The following pages will introduce you to specific examples of how you can make your tai chi practice more challenging. Let them serve as the springboard to your own creative methods of taking your practice to the next level.

Tai chi challenge

Yang 24 Short Form

The Yang 24 Short Form starts at 12 o'clock, and then you turn to face your centerline to 9 o'clock. There is plenty of variation in this tai chi form, bringing you through many different directions. This helps to develop your proprioception—or awareness of where you are in space. That spacial awareness is the gateway to further awareness, which the Taoists believe leads to true enlightenment.

1 Opening
pages 48–49

2a Wild Horse Parts Mane Left
pages 50–51

2b Wild Horse Parts Mane Right
pages 52–53

2c Wild Horse Parts Mane Left
pages 50–51

3 White Crane Spreads Wings
pages 54–55

8c Press Right
pages 80–81

8b Roll Back Right
pages 78–79

8a Grasp Sparrow's Tail: Ward Off Right
pages 76–77

7e Grasp Sparrow's Tail: Transition
pages 74–75

7d Grasp Sparrow's Tail: Push Left
pages 72–73

8d Push Right
pages 82–83

8e Transition
pages 84–85

9a Single Whip (Part one)
pages 86–87

9b Single Whip (Part Two)
pages 88–89

18b Fair Lady Threads Shuttles Left
pages 108–109

18a Fair Lady Threads Shuttles Right
pages 106–107

17 Snake Creeps Down and Golden Pheasant Stands on One Leg Right
pages 104–105

16 Snake Creeps Down and Golden Pheasant Stands on One Leg Left
pages 102–103

19 Needle at Sea Bottom
pages 110–111

20 Fan through the Back
pages 112–113

21a Turn Body and Deflect
pages 114–115

4 a Brush Knee and Twist Step Left
pages 56–57

4 b Brush Knee and Twist Step Right
pages 58–59

4 c Brush Knee and Twist Step Left
pages 56–57

5 Playing Pipa
pages 60–61

6 a Repulse Monkey Right
pages 62–63

6 b Repulse Monkey Left
pages 64–65

7 c Grasp Sparrow's Tail: Press Left
pages 70–71

7 b Grasp Sparrow's Tail: Roll Back Left
pages 68–69

7 a Grasp Sparrow's Tail: Ward Off Left
pages 66–67

6 d Repulse Monkey Left
pages 64–65

6 c Repulse Monkey Right
pages 62–63

10 a Cloud Hands (Part One)
pages 90–91

10 b Cloud Hands (Part Two and Part Three)
pages 92–93

11 a Single Whip (Part one)
pages 86–87

11 b Single Whip (Part Two)
pages 88–89

15 Turn Body and Kick Left Foot
pages 100–101

14 Double Strike Opponent's Ears
pages 98–99

13 Kick Right Foot
pages 96–97

12 High Pat on Horse
pages 94–95

21 b Parry and Punch
pages 116–117

22 Withdraw and Push
pages 118–119

23 Cross Hands
pages 120–121

24 Concluding Posture
pages 122–123

New Frame Cannon Fist

To let you get a flavor of traditional Chen Style tai chi, this sequence introduces you to an excerpt of the powerful Chen Style tai chi chuan form known as "New Frame Cannon Fist" or "Chen Second Routine." The form is so-named for its rhythmic martial stepping and striking patterns that mimic the acoustics of a firing cannon. This form is excellent for storing and cultivating more *qi* while increasing the plyometric capacities.

1 **Yellow Dragon Stirs Water, Right Side**
pages 126–127

4 **Kick with Left Heel**
pages 132–133

3 **Yellow Dragon Stirs Water, Left Side**
pages 130–131

2 **Yellow Dragon Transition**
pages 128–129

6 **Kick with Right Heel**
pages 136–137

7 **Turn Up Flowers from Sea Bottom**
pages 138–139

5 **Kick Transition**
pages 134–135

8 **Hidden Hand Punch**
pages 140–141

9 **Closing Posture**
pages 142–143

Advanced Balance Sequence I

This balance sequence uses the Chen Style postures Kick with Left Heel and Kick with Right Heel. You will be holding the postures longer, so be careful if you have any joint pain in your legs. All your body weight will be loaded onto one leg and sustained there for a few minutes. If your leg starts to shake, aim that trapped energy down from your hips, through your legs and out the center of the foot sole just as taught for the belly of the fingers (page 40). Doing this will develop very strong connective tissue and toned muscles. It will also help you increase your *qi* flow. This sequence also works with the Yang style postures Kick Right Foot (pages 96–97) and Kick Left Foot (pages 100–101). For an extra challenge, increase the amount of time you hold up your leg, increase the height at which you hold it, and try closing your eyes.

1 **Kick with Left Heel**
pages 132–133

The higher the lift, the deeper the root

Anytime you elevate your leg—such as in rooster stances or kicks—lift it a little higher and hold for a bit longer. To create yin and yang balance, remember that the higher you lift your leg, the deeper you have to sit into your *kua*. Combine this with closing your eyes to develop a superior state of balance.

2 **Kick with Right Heel**
pages 136–137

Put it together

1 Stand upright and progressively relax all the way down through your feet and into the floor. Shift your weight onto your right leg, and execute Kick with Left Heel. Hold the kick for a minimum of 30 seconds. Keep your breath released.

2 Release your left leg, and then bring it back into a rooster stance before returning it to the floor. Stretch out your legs if you feel any cramping or stiffness.

3 Execute Kick with Right Heel, holding the kick for a minimum of 30 seconds.

Advanced Balance Sequence II

The first balance sequence utilized a high stance. This balance sequence here works with a deeper stance that will put most of your leg muscles into eccentric contraction while bearing weight, especially since you will be moving throughout the sequence. Eccentric contraction means that there is lengthening in your muscles while bearing weight. In fact, most of tai chi's slow movements involve weight-bearing during stages of eccentric contraction, which leads to the greatest muscle strengthening. Because you will be moving slowly, this balance sequence is excellent for building strong stabilizer muscle function. It calls for you to repeatedly use the Yang Style Repulse Monkey posture. Repulse Monkey is also an excellent exercise because it uses your walking and running muscles in reverse, because you are stepping backward. This develops the muscular system, the nervous system, and the *qi* flow.

1 Repulse Monkey Right
pages 62–63

Proper preparation

Precede this sequence with the various stretches covered on pages 150–161 to prevent cramping. You may also use those stretches afterwards to clear lactic acid from your muscle tissues and stretch the fibers.

2 Repulse Monkey Left
pages 64–65

Put it together

1 Get into the Repulse Monkey posture, and then sink deeper and slightly raise the entire front empty foot off the floor. Hold this for a minimum of 60 seconds. As your balance and strength improves, you can hold it longer. Sink just a little deeper, until you start to shake a little.

2 Place your foot on the floor, and slightly raise your stance As you retract your front leg and arm in preparation for the next movement, move even slower. As you step your leg behind you, fully extend it and pause in this position before touching your toes to the floor. Note the tendency of your body to lean forward: fix it by straightening up and slightly tucking your pelvis. Lower yourself on your weighted leg.

3 Continue the movement, slower than the normal pace, repeating on the other side for as many repetitions as you desire.

Advanced Balance Sequence III

Your empty leg will not be extended for this one. This balance sequence employs the rooster stance before and after kicks, as featured prominently in the Yang Style Golden Pheasant Stands on One Leg posture. Remember to imagine that you are sitting while you are standing. Holding this position for a longer time not only increases your balance, but it also helps you record proper alignment into muscle memory. You can vary this exercise by rapidly switching between Golden Pheasant Stands on One Leg on the left side and then the right side, all the while aiming to keep your movement clean and very stable. This sequence also tones your abdomen.

1 Golden Pheasant Stands on One Leg Left
pages 102–103

Standing meditation

This posture can be used to reach an energetic balance as well. To do so, while holding the posture, imagine your spirit, will, and wisdom, like a light shining through you, rise up through the top of your head and into the sky. Also imagine the weight and substance of your body sinking deeply into the earth. The balancing point through which the skyward and earthbound vectors join is your dantian. Stay your mind and feeling on the dantian, which is neutral and peaceful. Practicing this way transforms this balance exercise into a Taoist standing meditation.

**2 Golden Pheasant Stands
on One Leg Right**
pages 104–105

Put it together

1 Get into the Golden Pheasant Stands on One Leg posture at the end of Yang Style's Snake Creeps Down and Golden Pheasant Stands on One Leg Left, and hold the end position.

2 Pay special attention to your alignment. Along with proper head and spinal alignment, keep your raised upper arm in line with your raised thigh. Hold the raised arm bent at the elbow approximately 90 degrees and the hold the raised leg bent at the knee at approximately 90 degrees. Let the toes drop down on the raised leg. Keep your fingers pointed up with *qi* gently stretched through the belly of the fingers. Hold this for a minimum of 60 seconds.

3 Release the rooster stance, and perform Golden Pheasant Stands on One Leg Right, following the same directions as for the left side. Hold this for a minimum of 60 seconds.

Plyometric Sequence I

Plyometric strength is a muscle's ability to exert its maximum force in as short a time as possible, with as much speed and power as possible. It is the "explosive" power of the muscle, which is responsible for activities such as jumping. Requiring physical strength, flexibility, and good proprioception, plyometric sequences are reserved for only those who have built a solid tai chi foundation and are in good athletic condition. Wear athletic footwear, and do not practice on a hard surface like concrete. When landing from any jumps, do so by expelling trapped air by saying *hahhh* and relaxing into the *kua* as if it were the suspension system of a vehicle. This sequence consists of rapidly moving through both sides of the Yang Style Snake Creeps Down and Golden Pheasant Stands on One Leg posture.

1 **Snake Creeps Down and Golden Pheasant Stands on One Leg Left**
pages 102–103

Stayed prepared

Use stretches before and after plyometric sequences to keep your body in top-notch condition.

2 Snake Creeps Down and Golden Pheasant Stands on One Leg Right
pages 104–105

Put it together

1 To begin the sequence, swiftly slide down into the Snake Creeps Down, squatting as low as possible into your tiger stance and then rapidly rise to the Golden Pheasant Stands on One Leg.

2 As your move through the posture, emphasize the plyometric action of going into the rooster stance of Golden Pheasant Stands on One Leg, aiming for excellent stability and balance at the same time. When you rise up, do so as if someone is pulling you up from the kua. This will engage your leg muscles in a way that protects the muscle fibers and strengthens the tendons.

3 After the sequence, stand in a narrow horse stance, breathing deeply, and progressively sink your weight and instill relaxation into your body.

Plyometric Sequence II

In its origin, tai chi chuan employed plyometric training. This is strongly evident in the original Chen Style forms and the older Yang styles, but it is becoming a lost feature in today's practice of tai chi chuan. Aside from developing the power of muscle contraction, plyometric tai chi sequences can also increase calorie burning, thereby aiding in fat loss. The Kick with Left Heel and Kick with Right Heel postures of the Chen Style New Frame Cannon Fist sequence lend themselves well to plyometric tai chi chuan training. You can also jump off the weighted leg as you kick with the other leg. When kicking and landing, ensure that you are not holding your breath.

1 Kick with Left Heel
pages 132–133

Mix it up

To increase your power, jump as high as you can off the non-kicking leg and land in a deep squat. Focus on landing accurately and softly. Varying the heights of your stance makes for a powerful workout rarely seen or taught in the tai chi world today. To add further variation, practice the same side several times in succession.

2 **Kick with Right Heel**
pages 136–137

2 **Kick Transition**
pages 134–135

Put it together

1 Execute Kick with Left Heel, kicking out swiftly as you thrust out your arms at the same time. Keep your elbows slightly bent instead of locking out the joint.

2 Lift your toes so that you can pivot on your left heel, inwardly rotating your right leg to execute to execute a twine step for a Kick Transition.

3 Continue on to Kick with Right Heel, and repeat as above for as many repetitions as you desire.

Plyometric Sequence III

This plyometric sequence is a variation of the Yang Style tai chi chuan postures Kick Right Foot and Kick Left Foot. To boost its fat-burning and strength-building capacity, you move rapidly from a low twine stance to a high kicking stance. Feel free to jump off the weighted leg while kicking to enhance the plyometric aspect of this sequence. After the kick, momentarily withdraw into a rooster stance. Rapidly alternate between the right and left sides. Make sure you are well stretched before you begin.

1 **Twine step**
pages 38–39

2 **Kick Right Foot**
pages 96–97

Cool down and recover

Be certain to end your plyometric tai chi work with a cool-down to quiet your *qi*. Do a few Yang Style moves, such as the Grasp Sparrow's Tail sequence on both sides to allow your *qi* to settle and your heart rate to slow down. Then get into a comfortable horse stance and progressively sink your weight and relax with square breathing. Doing this will not only hasten your recovery time, but it strengthens your *qi*.

5 Kick Left Foot
pages 100–101

3 Rooster stance
page 30

4 Twine step
pages 38–39

Put it together

1 Assume a deep twine stance with almost all your body weight on your left leg. Tuck your right knee behind your left leg. There will be some weight on the right foot with this extreme twine stance. Sit into the stance as low as you wish. Keep your body upright with your head and lower back in proper alignment.

2 Cross your right wrist outside of your left. Imagine there is a large sphere between your arms. Keep elbows down.

3 Push your left leg hard into the earth to raise upward. At the same time, rapidly kick out at an angle 45 degrees off your centerline. Extend your arms out as you kick, with your right arm in line with your right leg. Keep your elbows down and slightly bent.

4 After the kick, retract your arms and legs momentarily in to a rooster stance. Immediately drop your weight and step your right foot in front, into a twine stance. Repeat on the other side.

Plyometric Sequence IV

Most plyometric exercises emphasize jumping, but it is important to develop upper-body explosive muscular ability, along with lower-body power. The easiest and most effective way to do this is by moving through fast punching drills. At its core, tai chi is a martial practice. How then, can anyone match the speed of a fast opponent if he or she always practices slowly? Traditional tai chi chuan focuses on intensive body and mind conditioning. Beginning with correcting imbalances and healing injuries, building structural and energetic skills, and cultivating a focused mind, tai chi conditioning then progresses into the faster training sampled here. When you do this punching drill, let your whole body be the punch, and aim the energy to the belly of the fingers and the fist, and not just to the punching hand, but to the other one and the legs, as well.

Punch with style

Like your head and torso, your punching arm needs proper alignment. Keep your elbow down and slightly bent when you punch. Ensure that your wrist is straight, and tighten your fist at the real or imagined point of impact. Then, immediately loosen your fist and retract it. To improve your accuracy, hang a piece of paper from a string to serve as a target. To heighten your spirit, imagine you are punching through an obstacle in your life. See it shattering and dispersing like grains of sand. Punch several times with the same arm. As you punch, sit and slightly twist in your *kua* to give power to the punch.

Put it together

1 Start in a bow-and-arrow stance, and practice repeatedly punching. First punch with the hand opposite your forward leg. Punch and then retract. Repeat while aiming for speed and accuracy.

2 Jump to switch your stance into the opposite bow-and-arrow stance. Repeat as above.

Standing exercises

raditional tai chi chuan always employed standing exercises, some more meditative and others for *qi* development. Nonetheless, all standing exercises require excellent structure, relaxed breathing, and a mind always correcting itself to neutrality.

Standing exercises that employ horse stance are known as Zhang Zhuang, which roughly means to "stand like a stake." You envision your spine as a ridgepole holding your body in position and connecting it with the energy of the earth and the sky.

Standing exercises are intimidating—they take patience and strength. Still, anyone can do them to some degree; the amount of time and depth of stance does not matter. At

Stretch it out

Follow any standing exercise with a little bit of movement or some stretching. This will normalize your *qi* and blood circulation and make you feel pleasantly refreshed.

first you might hold a standing exercise for only 30 seconds while maintaining peace and focus, but your capacity will undoubtedly expand with practice. And as it does, so does your body strength, as well as your *qi* and mental strength.

When you are done, immediately do a few Upper-Back Release and Shoulder Release stretches (pages 154–155) to avoid soreness and stiffness from setting in.

Arms Made of Iron

The Arms Made of Iron exercise tones the upper body and helps make it feel light as a feather when you are done. Regular practice builds nicely toned arms while opening up the *qi* flow in your upper body. It also helps normalize your circulation if you have tend to have cold hands.

To execute Arms Made of Iron, grasp a pair of weights or cans of soup, one in each hand. Stand straight. Relax your chest inwardly and drop your shoulders.

Extend your arms straight out to your sides, but with your elbows down and relaxed. While you hold the position, press the energy from your shoulder down your arms and out the belly of your fingers into the weights.

Hold for five minutes or more, relaxing into the intensity. To hasten your toning and *qi* flow, grasp the heaviest weights you can hold out for about one to two minutes, or until your arms start to shake.

If you have a leg injury, or are otherwise impaired, you can do the Arms Made of Iron exercise sitting down.

Legs Made of Iron

You can do this excellent standing exercise virtually anywhere. To start, try it for a few minutes at a time. Depicted here is a deep, wide stance, but you can take a narrower, higher one until you are ready to go lower. The best way to develop your legs is to take as deep a stance as possible and hold until you feel your leg muscles shake a little bit. Doing this repeatedly, at least once a day, will give you what the Chinese call "legs made of iron."

Building up the stabilizing power of your legs with this exercise will lead to a high quality of life in your later years. As we age, our leg muscles and neuromuscular connections degenerate. This leads to weakness, stiffness, and the propensity to fall. Invest in making your legs strong. Then, as you age, you will have the legs and strength of a much younger person.

Double strength
Blend Legs Made of Iron and Arms Made of Iron—the two standing exercises make a powerful combination.

How to do it

To begin Legs Made of Iron, assume as deep a horse stance as possible, while still keeping your posture erect. If you have long legs, you will need to place your feet wider apart. If you are a woman, you may have to rotate your feet outwardly a bit to accommodate the extra flare of the female pelvis.

Bring up your arms in front of you, sink your shoulders, and keep your elbows down. Open your fingers. Imagine your arms and hands are relaxing around a large, light sphere.

Sit deeply and continuously instill your progressive sinking and relaxing actions.

When you sense intensity, breathe through it and relax into it. Maintain your position for one to five minutes to start, or until your legs begin to tremble. The more your mind resists the tension, the more it can benefit you as you learn to relax into the resistance, thereby making it vanish.

At completion, use the upper-leg stretches, Quadriceps Release and Biceps Femoris Release (pages 160), or use any other stretches that help you relax and remove stiffness before it can settle into your tissues. Keep well hydrated.

Create your own sequences

Tai chi chuan, at one time long ago, had no sets to memorize. It's just that the Chen style tai chi chuan forms are the oldest, fully documented sets of codified tai chi chuan forms. Before the Chen family clan, there has been historical evidence of tai chi chuan practice. At that time, it went by different names, such as *hua chuan* ("neutralizing" chuan), or long chuan, among others.

Building blocks of tai chi chuan
The early Tai Chi Classics (a collection of historical tai chi writings spanning several centuries by several authors) never make mention of memorizing a specific set of movements. Instead, these classics speak of various basic stances and energies that could be employed in numerous sets of movements. These martial and energetic qualities were named the "Eight Gates" and the "Five Steps." These are said to be the building blocks of tai chi chuan.

While a discussion of these sophisticated classical principles is beyond the scope of a book, it tells us an important fact: the self-development garnered from a tai chi practice is not obtained from memorizing a set of moves. Instead, it is obtained by a mindful application of the tai chi chuan

principles that govern all those tai chi movements. Merely collecting a bunch of tai chi postures in your memory and spewing them forth like a machine will give you little more than some basic stretching.

A strong foundation
Memorizing a tai chi form is important for giving you a foundation. Yet the purpose of any foundation is to build something on it. Committing your tai chi movements to memory is like burning a program to a computer's hard disk. You want clean coding and optimal function. Therefore, commit to doing your tai chi well instead of memorizing it quickly. Otherwise you will wind up undoing mistakes that got "programmed in" by not paying attention.

You cannot be a perfectionist either—if you are so afraid of making a mistake or doing something wrong, you will stay stuck. Again, you need a balanced approach, just as the concept of yin and yang teaches us. One way to "break" from the posture-collecting, mindless mentality is to take what tai chi postures you do know and rearrange them, creating your own form.

You don't have to write your form down. Let it flow out of you spontaneously—much like when jazz musicians get together for a jam session. They just let their music flow out while still following the principles of jazz. The jazz principles govern their music, yet allow them to be infinitely creative. And so it is with tai chi chuan.

Master the footwork
The secret to making it all flow out of you like water pouring down a mountain is in mastering the footwork. This does not mean you have to be a tai chi master, but you must have a good working knowledge of the tai chi footwork covered in the beginning of this book. Tai chi is just a few basic stances mixed with a plethora of different arm and hand positions. Look for curves and straight lines. Blend and mix. Be free. Get up now and try something!

Create time
If you are short on time, remember that 15 minutes of highly focused tai chi practice, steeped in tai chi principles, is far more conducive to your self-development than 90 minutes of "fluff" tai chi. Which tai chi postures address weaknesses you are trying to strengthen or imbalances you need to correct? Just work on those. Don't give in to an "all or nothing" extremist mentality. It does not matter if you cannot do the whole form or section of tai chi chuan. Just take a section and work on it.

Make a bad situation better

Exercise your creativity by thinking of all the ways you can engage tai chi principles when you are unable to find a time or place for practice. Are you stuck in a traffic jam, for instance? The common response is to meet the situation with frustration and tense posture. The Taoist point of view and a tai chi approach can turn a bad situation into a productive one: If you cannot get off the road and must stay on it to accomplish your goal of travel, then you need to change until it changes. Work on good posture. Head straight, ears in line with shoulders, no sway back. Work on keeping your chest drained and empty of tension and excess air.

In this situation, you could work on dantian compressions and expansions or deep breathing. This will clear your body and energy field as well as massage your internal organs. You can practice being at one with the sounds of the traffic, letting them flow through your awareness instead of getting stuck there. If you have a motivational recording or access to soothing music, play it. Now you have turned a time of frustration into a time of self-development.

Your unique form

Start with the opening posture of the Yang Style tai chi chuan. Once it's completed, or almost completed, you can do almost any step. Try an empty stance going into a twine step. Try a hook step. Can you put a half-step somewhere in there? A kick? Did you remember to rooster before and after the kick?

What would you like to do with your hands? Can you feel how your hands connect to your arms, which connect to your shoulders, which connects to your torso, which is centered at your dantian? If you can feel and move from the dantian, you have entered the level of whole-body skill, which is major progress in your tai chi development.

Try the arm positions you do know with different stances. Can you punch while in a horse stance? While going into a twine step, can you move your body so the arms look similar to their movements in White Crane Spreads Wings? Can you throw a back fist or parrying movement while doing a hook step that turns your body around? What breathing methods can you do while you practice? What empowering energies can you think up while doing variations on tai chi chuan movements? Can you swap out high stances for low ones and vice versa?

Explore your creativity

Like music and mathematics, the mind-body combinations of tai chi chuan are endless. Take your mind and body on a journey of exploring your creativity and growth in tai chi chuan. Stick to the standard forms for a solid foundation and familiar basis, but always feel free to experiment making variations. Just govern everything with good structure and balance. That's all you need.

Conclusion

Congratulations on your progress! And yes, even if you only have given it a little try thus far, you are different now. You have had a taste of tai chi. That knowledge and experience connects you to all the other people in the world who practice it. Across time and space, your newfound knowledge connects you with those tai chi masters and practitioners who came before you, those who will come after you, and those tai chi practitioners living on the other side of this planet.

This book introduces you to tai chi chuan from a more physical approach, with the emphasis on the joints and muscles. It is appropriate because tai chi is a highly kinesthetic art as much as it is a mental one. It is easy to get caught up in the philosophy and energy work of tai chi and forget that it can only make itself real by expressing through your physical body. By focusing on the basic locomotive system of your body, we bring the art back to earth.

Keep in mind too, that while tai chi works with the forces of physics acting on and from your body, it is an art. An art yields itself to infinite creativity, quality, and results. Use your tai chi practice as a gateway to physical self-development, as well as mental and spiritual self-development. Start with what you can understand and do, and go from there. That is the true meaning of a mind-body art. And as you gain greater self-awareness and physical cultivation, the right opportunities, teachings, and teachers will appear on your journey.

Websites

Because of the changing nature of Internet links, Rosen Publishing has developed an online list of websites related to the subject of this book. This site is updated regularly. Please use this link to access this list:

http://www.rosenlinks.com/FMB/Tai

Glossary

GENERAL TERMINOLOGY

acupressure: A practice of traditional Chinese medicine in which finger pressure into special "acupoints" on the body is said to balance the flow of *qi*, thereby resulting in decreased pain and increased health.

acupuncture: A practice of traditional Chinese medicine in which thin needles are lightly inserted into special "acupoints" on the body to balance the flow of *qi*, thereby resulting in decreased pain and increased health.

back heel line/back of the heel line: In an L-stance, an imaginary line perpendicular to the back of the heel of the base foot.

belly of the fingers: The first proximal phalanges, or base section of the fingers.

bow-and-arrow stance: A common tai chi stance that resembles a forward lunge.

Chen Style: The oldest codified form of tai chi chuan, which is deemed to be the origin of all tai chi forms.

chi (Wade-Giles): 1) the life-force energy. 2) the *chi* of "tai chi chuan" means "polarities." (pinyin = qi)

dantian (pinyin): Literally means "elixir field." The main dantian is the center of gravity and center of *qi* energy according to Taoist practices. (Wade Giles = tan tien)

empty stance: A tai chi stance in which all the body weight is on one leg. The leg holding no weight is said to be "empty."

gua sha: A bodywork methodology of traditional Chinese medicine that uses scraping techniques to release and balance *qi* flow.

half step: Bringing the back leg up near the front leg, and then stepping down on it.

holistic: Studying and working with the whole unit and interdependence of its components, instead of working on the components as separate units. For example, holistic health considers the entire mind-body-spirit aspects in the healing or development of an individual.

hook hand: A tai chi chuan hand position in which all five fingertips are drawn together and the wrist is fully flexed.

hook step: A tai chi moving stance in which a foot

is rotated internally from the hip, usually to turn the individual 180 degrees.

horse stance: The most common stance of all Chinese martial arts, qigong, and standing meditation practices. One of the first stances learned in tai chi.

internal alchemy: The Taoist approach to using special mental processes, exercises, and the internal chemistry of the body to attain specific health or spiritual goals.

kinesthetic: Pertaining to the ability to feel and understand movement. Related to the sense of touch.

kua: The hips; specifically, the inguinal crease; the V shape made where the torso joins the legs.

kung fu: 1) Chinese martial arts systems based on the philosophies of Buddhism and/or Confucianism. 2) Kung fu can also refer to any highly developed skill in any art. For example, a good calligrapher is said to have good kung fu of his calligraphy.

L-stance: A tai chi stance in which the feet upon the floor look like the letter L.

long form/traditional long form: A recognized set of traditional tai chi chuan, usually named after the surname of its progenitor. Most traditional long forms contain an average of 100 tai chi postures.

meridians: The lines of concentrated *qi* flow in which acupoints are located.

perineal area: The area on the body located between the anus and genitals.

pinyin: The method of romanization now used in China, all Chinese bilingual dictionaries, and taught in universities teaching Chinese as a foreign language.

pipa: A traditional Chinese lute-like instrument.

qi (pinyin): The basic life-force energy present in all beings as well as the universe, according to Taoist philosophy and traditional Chinese medicine. (Wade-Giles = chi, though different from the chi of "tai chi chuan")

qigong (pinyin): The practice of cultivating the life-force energy. Tai chi chuan utilizes qigong practices and techniques. (Wade-Giles = chi kung.)

rooster stance: A tai chi empty stance in which the knee is raised with the femur parallel to the floor.

Shifu: The Mandarin (standard) Chinese dialect word for "professional teacher."

short form: Any form of tai chi excerpted from a traditional long form of tai chi chuan. Lengths vary, but most usually contain fewer than 50 postures.

stances: The footwork of tai chi chuan. A term used interchangeably with "steps."

steps: The footwork of tai chi chuan. A term used interchangeably with "stances."

tai chi: 1) the shortened term for "tai chi chuan." 2) a term from Taoist philosophy that roughly translates to "great polarities" or "grand terminus" and describes the beginning of a state of change. (Pinyin = taiji)

tai chi chuan: A Chinese physical art, rooted in Taoism, which can be practiced martially and/or for health. (Pinyin = taijiquan)

Tai Chi Classics: A compendium of writings that may date as far back as the Song Dynasty (960–1279). The Tai Chi Classics do not list tai chi chuan forms, but instead the internal principles that must drive all tai chi chuan practice.

tai chi diagram: The curved teardrop shapes of two contrasting colors, symbolizing yin and yang. In Chinese it is called the *tai chi tu*.

tai chi principles: The energetic and structural principles that must drive all tai chi chuan forms for them to be considered the classical/traditional approach. The tai chi principles give power and maximum benefit to tai chi practice.

taijiquan: The pinyin Romanization of "tai chi chuan."

Tao: Means "The Way." The subject of study in Taoism.

Taoism: The oldest native philosophy of China. A way of studying nature and how we are a part of it.

tiger stance: A tai chi stance in which one squats body weight onto one leg and fully extends the other, with both feet rooted on the floor.

traditional Chinese medicine: The practice of acupuncture, bodywork, energy work, exercise, herbology, and other holistic methods used successfully in China for several thousands of years, to treat mind-body health (abbreviated TCM).

twine step: A tai chi moving stance in which the foot is rotated externally from the hip, pivoting on the heel. Also known as "sit stance," "cross-legged stance," or "lotus stance."

twist step: A tai chi moving stance in which the back foot pivots inward on the heel via internal rotation of the hip.

Wade-Giles: A now outdated method of romanization of the Chinese written language.

whole-body movement: Tai chi is classically classified as a whole-body movement. This means that the movement must originate in one's core and then spread to the periphery, and involve the entire body at every instant. Also known as "torso method."

whole step: Taking a complete step from back to front, as in walking.

Yang 24 Short Form: A globally recognized short form of tai chi chuan excerpted from the traditional Yang long form tai chi chuan.

Yang Cheng Fu: The last of the most famous of the Yang family masters. He standardized the traditional Yang long form tai chi chuan to what is commonly practiced today.

Yang Lu Chan: The progenitor of the Yang Style tai chi chuan, who pioneered a more open teaching and sharing of tai chi in China. He mastered tai chi under the Chen family in the 1700s.

Yang Style: The style of tai chi chuan accredited to Yang Lu Chan and his family. The most popular style of tai chi chuan.

yin and yang: A concept originating from Taoism that explains the harmony and interdependence of opposites. Symbolized by the tai chi diagram.

Zen Buddhism: An old Chinese sect of Buddhism originating in the sixth century. Zen is the common Japanese name, but "Chan" is the actual Chinese name for it. The original basis of most kung fu martial arts.

zhan zhuang: Literally means to "stand like a stake." A collection of standing meditation and qigong exercises to develop the body, spirit, and *qi*, and to hasten development in tai chi chuan practice.

Zhang San Feng: The legendary founder of the system of tai chi chuan, who lived between the Song and Ming dynasties and penned the first of the Tai Chi Classics.

LATIN TERMINOLOGY

The following glossary list explains the Latin terminology used to describe the body's musculature. In some instance, certain words are derived from Greek, which is therein indicated.

Chest

coracobrachialis: Greek *korakoeidés*, "ravenlike," and *brachium*, "arm"

pectoralis (major and minor): *pectus*, "breast"

Abdomen

obliquus externus: *obliquus*, "slanting," and *externus*, "outward"

obliquus internus: *obliquus*, "slanting," and *internus*, "within"

rectus abdominis: *rego*, "straight, upright," and *abdomen*, "belly"

serratus anterior: *serra*, "saw," and *ante*, "before"

transversus abdominis: *transversus*, "athwart," and *abdomen*, "belly"

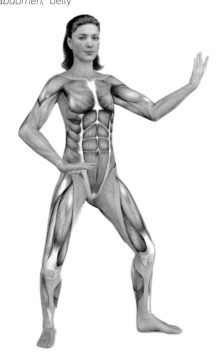

Neck

scalenus: Greek *skalénós*, "unequal"

semispinalis: *semi*, "half," and *spinae*, "spine"

splenius: Greek *spléníon*, "plaster, patch"

sternocleidomastoideus: Greek *stérnon*, "chest," Greek *kleís*, "key," and Greek *mastoeidés*, "breastlike"

Back

erector spinae: *erectus*, "straight," and *spina*, "thorn"

latissimus dorsi: *latus*, "wide," and *dorsum*, "back"

multifidus spinae: *multifidus*, "cut into divisions," and *spina*, "spine"

quadratus lumborum: *quadratus*, "square, rectangular," and *lumbus*, "loin"

rhomboideus: Greek *rhembesthai*, "to spin"

trapezius: Greek *trapezion*, "small table"

Shoulders

deltoideus (anterior, medial, and posterior): Greek *deltoeidés*, "delta-shaped"

infraspinatus: *infra*, "under," and *spina*, "thorn"

levator scapulae: *levare*, "to raise," and *scapulae*, "shoulder [blades]"

subscapularis: *sub*, "below," and *scapulae*, "shoulder [blades]"

supraspinatus: *supra*, "above," and *spina*, "thorn"

teres (major and minor): *teres*, "rounded"

Upper arm

biceps brachii: *biceps*, "two-headed," and *brachium*, "arm"

brachialis: *brachium*, "arm"

triceps brachii: *triceps*, "three-headed," and *brachium*, "arm"

Lower arm

anconeus: Greek *anconad*, "elbow"

brachioradialis: *brachium*, "arm," and *radius*, "spoke"

extensor carpi radialis: *extendere*, "to extend," Greek *karpós*, "wrist," and *radius*, "spoke"

extensor digitorum: *extendere*, "to extend," and *digitus*, "finger, toe"

flexor carpi pollicis longus: *flectere*, "to bend," Greek *karpós*, "wrist," *pollicis*, "thumb," and *longus*, "long"

flexor carpi radialis: *flectere*, "to bend," Greek *karpós*, "wrist," and *radius*, "spoke"

flexor carpi ulnaris: *flectere*, "to bend," Greek *karpós*, "wrist," and *ulnaris*, "forearm"

flexor digitorum: *flectere*, "to bend," and *digitus*, "finger, toe"

palmaris longus: *palmaris*, "palm," and *longus*, "long"

pronator teres: *pronate*, "to rotate," and *teres*, "rounded.

Hips

gemellus (inferior and superior): *geminus*, "twin"

gluteus maximus: Greek *gloutós*, "rump," and *maximus*, "largest"

gluteus medius: Greek *gloutós*, "rump," and *medialis*, "middle"

gluteus minimus: Greek *gloutós*, "rump," and *minimus*, "smallest"

iliopsoas: *ilium*, "groin," and Greek *psoa*, "groin muscle"

obturator externus: *obturare*, "to block," and *externus*, "outward"

obturator internus: *obturare*, "to block," and *internus*, "within"

pectineus: *pectin*, "comb"

piriformis: *pirum*, "pear," and *forma*, "shape"

quadratus femoris: *quadratus*, "square, rectangular," and *femur*, "thigh"

Upper leg

adductor longus: *adducere*, "to contract," and *longus*, "long"

adductor magnus: *adducere*, "to contract," and *magnus*, "major"

biceps femoris: *biceps*, "two-headed," and *femur*, "thigh"

gracilis: *gracilis*, "slim, slender"

rectus femoris: *rego*, "straight, upright," and *femur*, "thigh"

sartorius: *sarcio*, "to patch" or "to repair"

semimembranosus: *semi*, "half," and *membrana*, "skin or membrane"

semitendinosus: *semi*, "half," and *tendo*, "tendon"

tensor fasciae latae: *tenere*, "to stretch," *fasciae*, "band," and *latae*, "laid down"

vastus intermedius: *vastus*, "immense, huge," and *intermedius*, "between"

vastus lateralis: *vastus*, "immense, huge," and *lateralis*, "side"

vastus medialis: *vastus*, "immense, huge," and *medialis*, "middle"

Lower leg

adductor digiti minimi: *adducere*, "to contract," *digitus*, "finger, toe," and *minimum*, "smallest"

adductor hallucis: *adducere*, "to contract," and *hallex*, "big toe"

extensor digitorum: *extendere*, "to extend," and *digitus*, "finger, toe"

extensor hallucis: *extendere*, "to extend," and *hallex*, "big toe"

flexor digitorum: *flectere*, "to bend," and *digitus*, "finger, toe"

flexor hallucis: *flectere*, "to bend," and *hallex*, "big toe"

gastrocnemius: Greek *gastroknémía*, "calf [of the leg]"

peroneus: *peronei*, "of the fibula"

plantaris: *planta*, "the sole"

soleus: *solea*, "sandal"

tibialis anterior: *tibia*, "reed pipe," and *ante*, "before"

tibialis posterior: *tibia*, "reed pipe," and *posterus*, "coming after"

About the author

Shifu Loretta Wollering is a recognized expert and master-level tai chi instructor. She specializes in teaching tai chi from its traditional principles, and heads the traditional lineage of the late tai chi grandmaster Jou Tsung Hwa.

Wollering has more than 20 years of experience teaching and using tai chi chuan for health and inner peace, and she has the rare experience of using traditional tai chi's martial arts applications as well.

She makes regular media appearances, publishes works in trade magazines, and produces video. She has won numerous awards and honors and is a 2008 recipient of a leadership award from the President's Council on Physical Fitness and Sports (Washington, D.C.).

Wollering continues to pioneer promotion of tai chi through the Internal Gardens Tai Chi global online school of tai chi so that anyone, anywhere, can afford to benefit from this incredible practice: www.InternalGardens.com

Wollering is also the director of one of America's largest public conferences of tai chi chuan, Tai Chi Gala, held each year in June: www.TaiChiGala.com.

Acknowledgments

Special thanks to Grandmaster Jou Tsung Hwa for the gift of tai chi he shared with me, and special thanks to my parents for their support during the challenging times.

Credits

All photographs by Jonathan Conklin Photography, Inc., except:

Page 8 Jorg Hackemann/Shutterstock.com; 9 iBird/Shutterstock.com; 10 top left KUCO/Shutterstock.com; 10 bottom right windmoon/Shutterstock.com; 11 bottom middle Gisling/WikiCommons; 12 top right Sergii Figurnyi/Shutterstock.com; 12 bottom right Krisdayod/Shutterstock.com; 13 Simon Krzic/Shutterstock.com; 14 ostill/Shutterstock.com; 15 left Flashon Studio/Shutterstock.com; 15 right Ann Baldwin/Shutterstock.com; 16 left Juriah Mosin/Shutterstock.com; 16 right Paul Reeves Photography/Shutterstock.com; 17 Svetlana Larina/Shutterstock.com; 18 left Maxim Tupikov/Shutterstock.com; 18 middle Adisa/Shutterstock.com; 18 right Gayvoronskaya_Yana/Shutterstock.com; 19 Jack Z Young/Shutterstock.com; 20 Netfalls - Remy Musser/Shutterstock.com; 21 left Netfalls - Remy Musser/Shutterstock.com; 21 top right Madlen/Shutterstock.com; 21 bottom right Dionisvera/Shutterstock.com; 22 left Janet Faye Hastings/Shutterstock.com; 22 middle SOMMAI/Shutterstock.com; 22 top right Dionisvera/Shutterstock.com; 22 bottom right Drozdowski/Shutterstock.com; 23 top left oriori/Shutterstock.com; 23 middle left Kelvin Wong/Shutterstock.com; 23 top right Charlotte Lake/Shutterstock.com; 23 bottom right Stuart Jenner/Shutterstock.com; 24 left Billy Quinn/MoonToad NL/flickr.com; 25 left Cyril Hou/Shutterstock.com; 26 Steve Scott/Shutterstock.com; 27 Vadim Ivanov/Shutterstock.com; 28 Franck Boston/Shutterstock.com; 40 elwynn/Shutterstock.com; 41 defpicture; 42 Vitaliy Netiaga/Shutterstock.com; 43 middle Hintau Aliaksei/Shutterstock.com; 43 right AGorohov/Shutterstock.com; 146 Mahesh Patil/Shutterstock.com; 147 jamie cross/Shutterstock.com; 153 right Kosarev Alexander/Shutterstock.com; 186–87 iBird/Shutterstock.com.

All anatomical illustrations by Hector Aiza/3 D Labz Animation India, except:

Small insets and full-body anatomy pages 45–45 by Linda Bucklin/Shutterstock.com; page 25 middle, 153 left design36/Shutterstock.com; pages 29, 30, 151, 152, 154, 156, 158, 160, 161 Sebastian Kaulitzki/Shutterstock.com; page 38 sam100/Shutterstock.com.